Who Is Jesus?

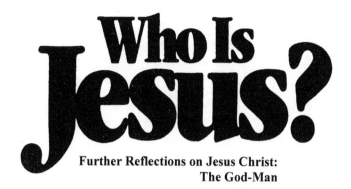

Who Is Jesus?

**Further Reflections on Jesus Christ:
The God-Man**

Bruce A. Demarest

Wipf & Stock
PUBLISHERS
Eugene, Oregon

Wipf and Stock Publishers
199 W 8th Ave, Suite 3
Eugene, OR 97401

Who Is Jesus?
Further Reflections on Jesus Christ: The God-Man
By Demarest, Bruce A.
Copyright©1984 by Demarest, Bruce A.
ISBN 13: 978-1-55635-420-5
ISBN 10: 1-55635-420-7
Publication date 4/10/2007
Previously published by Victor Books, 1984

Contents

1 Who Is Jesus?   7
2 Preexistent One   18
3 "God of God"   28
4 God Become Man   39
5 Offspring of Mary   50
6 The Unique God-Man   61
7 Master Teacher   72
8 Model Servant   83
9 Prophet, Priest, and King   93
10 Dying Saviour   103
11 Resurrected Lord   113
12 Seated Sovereign   123

1

Who Is Jesus?

A Hindu principal once asked a Christian schoolgirl in India why she refused to sing the praises of Krishna when the Hindu girls were quite happy to join in the singing of *All Hail the Power of Jesus' Name*. The girl tried to explain, but finally blurted out, "I can't sing to anyone but Jesus!" This was her way of saying that Christianity is more than a creed; it is a living *Person*. W. H. Griffith Thomas once made the point in the title of a popular book, *Christianity Is Christ*.

In this respect Christianity is unique among the world's faiths. The most important thing about Buddhism is not Gautama the Buddha, but his teachings. Or to take a Western religion, Mormonism makes no claim to worship Joseph Smith; it is simply following his instruction in *The Book of Mormon*. The significant feature about the Christian faith, however, is not the Sermon on the Mount —as great as this may be—but the person of Jesus Christ in all His grandeur. Christianity is centrally concerned with the worship of a Person.

Remarkably, the name of Jesus has become a household word in our day. We confront His name daily on bumper stickers, billboards, the Broadway stage, popular news magazines, even the *Wall Street Journal*. Perhaps not since the days of the early church has Jesus been the object of such intense interest. Tim Rice and

Andrew Webber, who do not claim to be Christians, told what caused them to write the popular rock opera, *Jesus Christ Superstar.* "Wouldn't a musical on the life of Christ be great," they said, "because this is . . . definitely . . . the most famous and interesting life story of all."

Jesus' popularity is all the more remarkable since humanly speaking His life was so commonplace. The statement, "One Solitary Life" says it well.

He was born in an obscure village, the child of a peasant woman. He grew up in another village, where He worked in a carpenter shop until He was thirty. Then for three years He was an itinerant preacher. He never wrote a book. He never held an office. He never had a family or owned a home. He didn't go to college. He never visited a big city. He never traveled two hundred miles from the place where He was born. He did none of the things that usually accompany greatness. He had no credentials but Himself.

Although unnoticed and unheralded, Jesus has done more than any other man to shape human history. The division of time into years B.C. and A.D. testifies to this impact. His ethical teachings are imbedded in the world's noblest social and political institutions. The world pauses at Christmas to celebrate His birth. Charles H. Spurgeon, the well-known English preacher, once said that "Christ is the great central fact in the world's history. To Him everything looks forward or backward. All the lines of history converge upon Him."

Spurgeon's fellow countryman, the essayist Charles Lamb, once observed, "If Shakespeare should come into this room, we would all rise; but if Jesus Christ should come in, we would all kneel." Surely, Jesus Christ is incomparable. The 60,000 books written about Him in the past century confirm that.

The Source of Our Knowledge

In his book *Jesus and Christian Origins outside the New Testament,* F. F. Bruce remarks that secular historians of Jesus' time paid little attention to Him. The crucifixion of a Jewish prophet on the fringe of the Empire would hardly make the headlines of the major dailies in the Roman world. Not until the Christian movement gained strength and riots broke out did historians sit up and take notice. As a result, after more than 1,900 years our main sources for the life and teachings of Jesus remain the four Gospels. If we want to determine what Jesus was like, we must turn to the Gospels.

During the past hundred years, however, the validity of the Gospels has come under attack. Some skeptics argue that idealistic Christians wrote the exaggerated reports in the Gospels simply to further the Christian cause. According to these critics, only the most meager connection exists between the real Jesus and the portrait of Him in the Gospels. Faith and history are separated by a wide chasm.

This sort of depreciation of the Gospels led some 19th-century liberal theologians to question whether Jesus ever lived at all. A German skeptic named Bruno Bauer (d. 1882) charged that Jesus never existed; the New Testament figure was simply the free creation of the religious genius (not Mark) who wrote the second Gospel. Even today many liberals believe that the Gospels provide little factual data about Jesus of Nazareth. One modern European theologian claims, for example, that the only authentic knowledge of Jesus in the Gospels is His death under Pontius Pilate.

In spite of the critics, however, Christianity remains wed to historical truth. Jesus' birth in Bethlehem was linked to a census ordered by Caesar Augustus. His death at Jerusalem was ordered at the pleasure of Pontius Pilate. If, as the French thinker Renan says, "all history is incomprehensible without Christ," the reverse is also true: Christ is incomprehensible apart from His historical context. A Christ isolated from the flow of history would be no different from the rising and dying gods of the Eastern mystery cults. Christianity without a real historical Jesus would make about as much sense as the Victorian Age without Queen Victoria.

In God's wisdom the four Gospels provide us with the information we need to conclude that Jesus was a real historical personality. The writers Matthew, Mark, Luke, and John wrote as those who had intimate knowledge of Jesus' life and teachings. But strictly speaking, their accounts are neither biographies nor histories. Neither are they handbooks of Christian doctrine.

The Gospels are a unique literary form unparalleled in the ancient world. They are selective portraits which accurately record the high points of Jesus' life and teachings, but they do so without presenting strictly chronological records. Guided by the Spirit, the Gospel writers apparently were free to arrange their material in such a way as would enhance in the best way the master plan of their work.

Matthew arranged Jesus' words and deeds topically in five major blocks to prove that Jesus fulfilled the Old Testament messianic hope. Mark, who was Peter's interpreter, may have written his Gospel after the pattern of Peter's preaching in Acts to persuade pagan Romans that Jesus was the Servant of God. Luke, the painstaking historian, arranged his account in chronological order (Luke 1:3) to commend Jesus to Gentiles. Likewise, the material available to John was chosen so as to uphold Jesus as the Christ, the Son of God (John 20:31). Under the direction of the Holy Spirit, the Gospel writers set forth in distinct but complementary ways the saving significance of Jesus Christ.

This view of the Gospels acknowledges that the documents were written by Jesus' committed followers from the perspective of faith. After the Evangelists had come to Christ, they wrote their Gospels in order to introduce Him to others. This commitment of faith does not destroy the integrity of the Gospel accounts, as some critics charge, because most historians recognize that the writing of history as "brute fact" is impossible. Every assessment of the past involves not only the collection of data and the selection of a suitable context into which the facts fit, but also an interpretation or explanation of the evidence. The Evangelists sought to determine not only "What happened?" but also "Why did it happen?" They recorded not only the details of Jesus' death, but also its significance in God's plan of salvation.

We conclude, then, that the Gospels offer a solid basis for the conviction that God was savingly at work in the life and ministry of Jesus of Nazareth. It may not be possible to marshall historical evidence which will provide 100 percent certainty on this matter. Nevertheless, in the Gospels we find historical evidence which is little short of remarkable. As Pascal astutely observed, in the Gospels "there is enough light for those who only wish to see, and enough darkness for those who are oppositely inclined."

"Who Do Men Say . . . ?"

Having weighed the historical reliability of the Gospels we now face the crucial question of Jesus' identity. Perhaps no more urgent issue confronts modern man than the question, "What do you think of Christ?" (Matt. 22:42) Dietrich Bonhoeffer, the German martyr, once remarked: "What is bothering me incessantly is the question . . . who Christ really is, for us today." While no figure is more highly esteemed than Jesus, no one is more frequently misunderstood than the Carpenter from Nazareth.

At the heart of Matthew's Gospel we find Jesus' encounter with Peter near Caesarea Philippi (Matt. 16:13ff.). In an attempt to instill a deeper awareness of His dignity prior to His fatal rendezvous in Jerusalem, Jesus posed to His followers the familiar question, 'Who do men say that the Son of man is?" Matthew notes that many rumors about Jesus' identity were circulating. Some held that He was John the Baptist returned from the dead. Others that He was Elijah come back to life in fulfillment of Malachi's promise (Mal. 4:5). Still others felt that He was Jeremiah or another Old Testament prophet. Clearly Jesus was someone special, but people disagreed as to who He was.

On other occasions popular opinion was not nearly as flattering. John tells us that people believed that Jesus was a Sabbath-breaker (John 5:16), a revolutionary (John 7:12), one demon-possessed (John 7:20; 8:48), or a sinner (John 9:24) of questionable origin (John 7:27). Matthew recalls that Jesus was accused of being a glutton and a drunkard (Matt. 11:19). Luke recalls that those who witnessed Jesus' deeds confessed, "We have seen strange things today" (Luke 5:26, KJV). To many of His contemporaries Jesus was an enigma. Paul's cry on the road to Damascus—"Who are You, Lord? (Acts 22:8, NIV)—echoes through the years, demanding a response from every person.

In reply to our Lord's probing question, Peter confessed that Jesus was more than a great religious teacher or prophet. He was in truth "the Christ, the Son of the living God" (Matt. 16:16)—

the personal, visible expression of Israel's God in human flesh. At best, other men called Jesus good. Peter alone confessed Him as God.

Many Things to Many Men

Since many who knew Jesus in the flesh were unsure of His identity, it is not surprising that confusion surrounds the person of Christ in the modern world. During the past 200 years the liberal tradition has regarded Jesus as little more than a man. Here was a Galilean peasant, a man of gentleness and humility, who lived as an itinerant preacher. He came to cross-purposes with the authorities and was arrested and disposed of with the consent of imperial Rome. His idealistic followers later made extravagant claims about Him alleging, of all things, that He was Israel's Messiah, the long-awaited One.

Liberal commentators went to great lengths to explain away the evidences of the miraculous in our Lord's ministry. Jesus' so-called miracles of healing were due to secret curative medicines. He never quieted a violent storm on the sea; His boat merely entered the shelter of a hill. He never fed the crowd by multiplying five loaves of bread and two fish; many onlookers simply followed His sacrificial example and shared what food they had. Jesus did not die on the cross; He was drugged and later revived in the coolness of the tomb. And so on.

Contemporary liberals are hardly more constructive. The Galilean prophet, they say, is merely one of many great religious figures in the world. The man Jesus is called "God" because His relationship with the Almighty was unique. A later generation of zealous Christians added to His simple humanity the mythical garments of preexistence, incarnation, and resurrection.

Clearly, both the older and newer forms of liberalism are opposed to biblical supernaturalism. Both are guided by the rationalism which accepts only what is consistent with the law of cause and effect in a closed system. Any violation of the assured results of science, such as the descent of God to earth in human form, or the union of humanity and divinity in a man, is judged as an ancient myth.

Contemporary variations on this basic liberal portrait of Jesus are legion. It is fashionable today to represent Jesus as the model humanitarian. Rather than think of our Lord as the remote God "out there," Dietrich Bonhoeffer focused on Christ's "being there for others." The important point is not the issue of Christ's "deity," but His concrete relation to the human community as "the man for others."

In recent years the English rock opera, *Jesus Christ Superstar,* has created fresh interest in the life of Jesus. Repeatedly the opera's chorus raises the question, "Who are you?" The developing plot focuses on Jesus' manhood. Pilate taunts the Lord, "Prove to me that you're divine—change my water into wine," and, "Prove to me that you're no fool—walk across my swimming pool." Simon the Zealot found in Jesus the markings of a revolutionary; Mary saw a person of extraordinary character; and the raucous crowd discovered a Superstar. The musical highlights Jesus' alleged sexual temptations, the agony of His sufferings, the disillusionment of shattered expectations. The plot thickens: "Jesus Christ Superstar, do you think you're what they say you are?" All is silence. The opera closes with Superstar in the grave.

In another recent sketch of Jesus, the Jewish writer Hugh Schonfield portrays the Nazarene as the principal actor in the *Passover Plot.* His story goes like this: Born in an era aglow with messianic fervor, Jesus really believed that He was Israel's Messiah. Skillfully, Jesus set the stage for the greatest plot in history: His baptism by John, the wilderness sojourn, the selection of 12 disciples, the details of His ministry in the land, the momentous events in Jerusalem. All were masterfully engineered to conform with the blueprint of Old Testament prophecy.

The climax of the plot in Jerusalem was crucial. Jesus deliberately allowed Himself to be trapped in the struggle between Pilate and the chief priests. He carefully laid the ground for Judas' betrayal. And when on the cross he signaled, "I thirst," a swoon-inducing drug was given Him. According to plan a fellow conspirator, Joseph of Arimathea, obtained Jesus' body, placed it in a tomb, and had it removed secretly at night. Later, Jesus died from His wounds and was buried in a secret grave. The plot engineered by Jesus cost Him His life. But it succeeded in that the ideals of selflessness, love, and resurrection live on.

A generation ago, in the popular book, *The Man Nobody Knows,* Bruce Barton depicted Jesus as the successful Madison Avenue business executive. Jesus was a poor Jewish lad who soon learned that the name of the game is "success." The rugged outdoorsman with features hard and clean and nerves of steel became the leader of a nondescript group of 12 men. Through the strength of His convictions, the leader's gift for developing the latent talents of His subordinates, and His efficient management skills, Jesus molded the group into an invincible organization which quickly spanned the Roman Empire. Jesus' message to others was what carried the day for Him: "Nothing is impossible if only your willpower is strong enough."

More recent events in the turbulent 20th century have given the concept of a militant Jesus a fresh popularity. The suggestion that Jesus was a political revolutionary, however, is by no means new. Some in our Lord's day saw Him in this light. Later, Rousseau, the 18th-century thinker whose ideas contributed to the French Revolution, held that Jesus was a social revolutionary whose primary purpose was to free the Jews from Rome's tyrannical rule. In a similar way, George Bernard Shaw, in the preface to *Androcles and the Lion,* claimed that Jesus was "a rallying center for revolutionary influence" in Roman Palestine.

It is true that in Jesus' day the Zealots were a group of armed insurrectionists whose political activities led to the fatal Jewish war against Rome (A.D. 66-70). That is why many people today claim that Jesus belonged to this Zealot party. After all, was not one of Jesus' followers Simon the Zealot?

From these ideas the so-called "theology of liberation" has emerged. Just as Jesus' mission was one of political liberation, so today, we are told, the church exists to free the socially enslaved from the shackles of oppression. Some liberationists believe that if Jesus were alive today He would be a revolutionary-minded Marxist.

Contemporary black theology, which weds black consciousness with liberation ideals, represents Jesus as a black Messiah bent on revolution. Albert Cleage in his book, *The Black Messiah,* bluntly claims that "Jesus was a revolutionary black leader, a Zealot, seeking to lead a Black Nation to freedom" from the tyranny of white Rome. Jesus highlights the essential "blackness" of the Gospel and helps to break the shackles placed on black people by the white oppressor.

Finally, we may recall that a few years ago the noted British Dead Sea Scroll scholar John Allegro, wrote an infamous book entitled, *The Sacred Mushroom and the Cross.* From his study of mushroom fungi, Allegro insists that the phenomena associated with Jesus in the Gospels correspond to the main features of an Eastern drug-sex cult which venerated the mushroom. According to the author, Jesus was the hero in the sacred mushroom mythology, and the cross was a symbol for the sexual activity prominent in the cult's worship. Fortunately Allegro's book has been roundly condemned by right-minded people of various persuasions.

What more shall we say? The theories have no end. Albert Schweitzer saw in Jesus a deluded apocalyptic visionary. Hitler found an Aryan who proved the superiority of Gentiles of European stock. Picasso pictured a dashing bullfighter. Spiritism presents Jesus as a pantheistic god. And the Baha'i faith portrays Him as one of nine human messengers. The modern portraits of Jesus appear to be without number.

Mystery, Revelation, and Christ

Times have changed very little in 2,000 years. John declares that Jesus, the Creator of the universe and the light of the world, has invaded this earthly scene. And although Jesus lived and walked among men, John concludes that "the world did not know Him" (John 1:10). Although Jesus openly manifested Himself, He was hidden to all but the eyes of faith.

The reason Jesus has often been misunderstood is that the person of our Lord—humanity and deity united in the God-man—is properly a spiritual mystery. The Apostle Paul quoted an early Christian confession sung in praise of Jesus Christ: "Great indeed, we confess, is the mystery of godliness: He was revealed in the flesh, vindicated in the Spirit" (1 Tim. 3:16).

Mystery involves a set of claims which from a human perspective appears contradictory but which from the divine perspective is perfectly consistent. The human mind cannot understand how the infinite God and finite man can be united in a single person, but before God the Christian is responsible to proclaim the mysteries of the faith, and only later attempt to solve its problems.

In His conversation with the disciples at Caesarea Philippi, Jesus indicated that faith rests upon revelation. In response to Peter's bold confession of Jesus as Messiah and Son of God, our Lord replied with profound approval: "Blessed are you, Simon Barjonas, because flesh and blood did not reveal this to you, but My Father who is in heaven" (Matt. 16:17). Our Lord's words confirm that the confession of Christ is possible only in the light of divine revelation. Only God can show a person what he ought to believe about Jesus Christ!

Scripture and history teach that any attempt to explain the essential mystery of Jesus Christ apart from divine revelation is doomed to failure. Paul said as much to the Corinthian believers: "No one can say 'Jesus is Lord,' except by the Holy Spirit" (1 Cor. 12:3). First, our answer to the question "Who is Jesus Christ?" is the answer of faith. This faith rests on God's testimony to His Son as recorded in Holy Scripture. Our estimate of Christ is based not upon shifting human opinion but upon the secure foundation of God's truthful Word. Second, our reply is the reply of obedience. Those who obey Him shall learn in their experience who He is. Faith and obedience declare, "Here is the Son of God and Saviour of the world!"

Jesus Christ and Salvation

Jesus' identity is more than a theoretical matter. Who Jesus Christ is relates profoundly to our salvation. As Peter proclaimed in an early sermon in Jerusalem, "there is salvation in no one else" (Acts 4:12). For John also, commitment to Jesus as the Son of God is necessary for salvation (1 John 5:11-12). Paul made the same point in his letter to the Romans: "If you confess with your mouth 'Jesus is Lord' . . . you will be saved" (Rom. 10:9). He who acknowledges that Jesus is *kyrios* (the Greek form of an

Old Testament name for God) is prepared to receive God's offer of salvation. A Christian, then, is a person who sees Jesus not as a moral teacher, an ethical prophet, or a Superstar, but the very Son of God in human form.

Yes, who Jesus is really matters. In the first place, Jesus Christ must be authentic man. A Greek phantom god would not do. If Jesus would properly take our place and bear our sins He must have been as fully human as we (Heb. 2:14). He must identify with the brokenhearted and the outcasts in the depth of their need. He must be one with the race He came to save.

But Jesus also must be fully God. Only an infinite sacrifice could bear the sins of the world. Malcolm Muggeridge sums it all up this way: "As Man alone, Jesus could not have saved us; as God alone He would not; Incarnate, He could and did."

John Calvin once said that "our iniquities, like a cloud intervening between Him and us have utterly alienated us from the kingdom of heaven. None but a person reaching to Him could be the medium of restoring peace." Jesus Christ can be thought of as a bridge between God and man which spans the chasm caused by sin (1 Tim. 2:5). To serve its intended purpose a bridge must be securely anchored on both ends.

At Avignon in Southern France, a bridge was built across the Rhone River. One end of the old bridge was inadequately secured, so that at a time of flood water it was swept away. With only half the structure intact the bridge was useless for crossing the Rhone. To this day a popular saying survives: "On the bridge of Avignon they dance in circles." If Christ did not possess perfect oneness with God and perfect solidarity with man, we sinners would be consigned to dancing aimlessly in circles rather than moving confidently to God through Jesus Christ, God's appointed Mediator.

2

Preexistent One

During His public ministry, at the close of one of the Feasts of Tabernacles—the week-long festival celebrating the end of the fruit harvest—Jesus stood and taught openly in the temple. In one of the ceremonies of the Feast, four great golden candelabra were lit to commemorate the pillar of fire which guided Israel through the wilderness at night. In the midst of this solemn service Jesus spoke out with clear, steady voice: "I am the light of the world" (John 8:12).

Before the assembled throng Jesus went on to claim that His origin was not of this world; He proceeded from the Father in heaven. Angered at Jesus' audacity, the Pharisees cried out, "Where is Your Father?" (v. 19) "Unlike you," they boasted, "we were not born of fornication" (v. 41).

In response to Jesus' claim that He came forth from God, the Jews snorted, "Surely You are not greater than our father Abraham" (v. 53). Jesus' answer to the calloused Pharisees was devastatingly simple: "Before Abraham was, I AM" (v. 58).

Notice, Jesus made the staggering claim that He, a man, preexisted the patriarch Abraham who lived 2,000 years earlier. Moreover, Jesus applied to Himself the sacred Old Testament name of Yahweh: "I AM WHO I AM" (Ex. 3:14). By so doing our Lord claimed an existence which was timeless. There was a

time when Abraham was not. But there never was a time when the
Son of God was not. He knows no past nor future. The Jews at the
feast well knew that Jesus claimed to be the eternal God, for
they immediately picked up stones to kill Him.

Defining the Issue

Preexistence is probably difficult for Westerners to understand.
People from the East are not so baffled by the concept. The
average Hindu believes that a person has had a prior existence in
a different form. And at death his soul will reincarnate itself in
yet another living form.

Centuries before Christ, Socrates and Plato also believed in the
preexistence of the soul. Later Judaism was influenced by these
Greek ideas. The Jews believed that everything of value had prior
existence in the mind of God. Thus the Law, the temple, and even
Moses had a kind of preexistence.

But Christ's preexistence is entirely different from the Greek
or Hindu ideas. No mere idea or "ideal" in the mind of God, the
eternal Son was a real person who revealed Himself during human
history in the man Jesus.

By Christ's preexistence, then, we mean that His personal
existence had its beginning not at His conception or birth, but in
the distant reaches of eternity past. As J. Oswald Sanders observes
in his book *The Incomparable Christ,* "His birth in Bethlehem
was not His origin, only His incarnation."

The man Jesus was absolutely unique. He is the only person in
history whose beginning was not marked by His birth. He had His
origin not in Mary's womb, but in the timelessly eternal being
of God. As someone put it so well, Jesus Christ is the Son of God
"with a prologue of eternal history and an epilogue of the same."

An ancient Latin inscription carved in marble expresses the
prior existence of the Lord Jesus Christ thus:

I am what I was—God.
I was not what I am—Man.
I am now called both—
GOD and MAN.

The doctrine of Christ's preexistence is enormously significant in the Christian scheme of truth. Thomas Carlyle hinted at this when he said, "He who has no vision of eternity has no hold on time."

What would result if the prior eternity of Christ were invalidated? Simply that the Christian faith as we know it would cease to exist. Without the preexistent Son antedating time there would be no Trinity. The God of the Bible and the church would vanish. Deny Christ's prior existence and there would be no incarnation of the Word. Negate preexistence and there would be no ultimate revelation of the Father. Jesus then would be no more significant as the source of revelation than Joseph Smith. Eliminate Christ's preexistence and the Atonement would be null and void. Only God can redeem a person. For good reasons, then, the eternal existence of Jesus Christ has been upheld as a key doctrine of Christianity.

Mistaken Ideas

Because of Christ's place in the Trinity the doctrine of His preexistence came under attack early. Arius (d. 336), a deacon in the church of Alexandria, worshiped Christ and held to a sort of preexistence. But Arius wrongly believed that the Son was a being fashioned in time, the first of God's created order. Although Christ was prior in time and superior in rank to all other creatures, His coeternity with the Father in the triune Godhead was denied.

During the period of the Reformation a group known as the Socinians held that Jesus was an ordinary man. As the reward of His perfect obedience, God "deified" Jesus by raising Him from the dead. One is mistaken, the Socinians argued, to think of Christ existing prior to His birth in Bethlehem.

Martin Luther wisely observed that the periodic reappearance of heretical views about Christ is not surprising. "I know nothing about the Lord Christ that the devil has failed to attack; that is why he must now start out again from the beginning and bring out the old errors and heresies."

American Unitarianism, led by such figures as Ralph Waldo Emerson, flatly denied the Trinity and the eternal existence of Christ. It is no surprise, then, to discover that in recent years many Unitarians have merged with the Universalist movement, which holds that all men will someday somehow be saved.

The Jehovah's Witnesses also reject Christ's eternal pre-existence. Jehovah's first act was to create the Son. Thus Christ was not eternal, but the firstborn among men. Before His appearance on earth Christ was actually the archangel Michael. Jesus was nothing but a man, and men do not preexist.

Mormonism teaches that prior to Bethlehem Jesus Christ was one of a host of preexistent spirits which included men and devils. Christ was not properly God; He was merely the firstborn of the spirit-children of God. Plainly, then, Mormonism denies the uniqueness and eternity of our Lord Jesus Christ.

Liberal Protestants also reject the supernaturalism of Christ's eternal preexistence. They attempt to explain away the biblical teaching in various ways. Many liberals claim that Christ is pre-existent in the sense that God appointed Jesus to His particular role in life before the foundation of the world. This line of thinking simply makes "preexistence" mean God's foreordination.

Other liberal Protestants see in the doctrine of preexistence a vestige of pagan mythology. Embedded in the myth, however, is the existential truth that "it is *God* with whom we have to do in Jesus." In the end, the concept of Christ's preexistence, like His deity, means very little at all to modern, "enlightened" man.

These false ideas must not be confused with the biblical doc-trine of the eternal generation of the Son. The Psalmist records the saying of Yahweh, "You are My Son, today I have begotten You" (Ps. 2:7, RSV). Jesus Himself declared, "as the Father has life in Himself, even so He gave to the Son also to have life in Himself" (John 5:26; see 1 John 5:18).

This idea that Jesus was "begotten" was expressed in the early creeds of the Church. The old Athenasian Creed, for example, reads in part: "The Son is from the Father alone, neither made, nor created, but begotten."

But how should we interpret the idea of the "begetting" of the Son? How does it differ from the false notions of the Arians or the Jehovah's Witnesses? Look at it this way. Back in eternity, the personal subsistence of the Son was brought forth from the reality of God. It was not the essence of the Son which came into being, but His personhood as a member of the Trinity. Calvin put it this way: "God did not choose to have life hidden and buried within Himself. Rather He poured it into His Son that it might flow to us."

This generation or begetting of the Son, we quickly add, was not from anything else; nor was it from nothing. God in eternity past communicated Himself to the Son. The Son originated from the Father's own being. More than this we cannot say. Ultimately the Father's begetting of the Son must be regarded as a mystery.

Old Testament Intimations

The Word of God is clear regarding Christ's eternal preexistence. J. Oswald Sanders rightly claims that the preexistence of our Lord "is nowhere in Scripture argued as a doctrine, but is everywhere assumed." Let us examine first the Old Testament teaching on this important issue.

The eighth chapter of Proverbs paints a remarkable portrait of wisdom. Solomon, himself a man of great wisdom, wrote: "The Lord possessed Me in the beginning of His way, before His works of old. I was set up from everlasting, from the beginning, as ever the earth was. . . . When He prepared the heavens, I was there. . . . When He appointed the foundations of the earth; then I was by Him; as one brought up with Him: and I was daily His delight, rejoicing always before Him" (Prov. 8:22-31, KJV).

The initial phrase, "The Lord possessed me at the beginning" has long been an object of debate. Back in the fourth century the Arians claimed that the word translated "possessed" in most versions ought to be rendered "created." Then Proverbs 8:22 would read, "The Lord created Me," proving that Christ, the wisdom of God, was a person created in time. The better translation, "possessed," in fact, suggests the exact opposite of the Arian argument. Possession is closely related to parenthood. Wisdom was not created by God; wisdom stands in a filial relation to God as one begotten by Him. Some authorities, indeed, translate the phrase in question as, "the Lord begot Me."

Nevertheless, it is clear from Proverbs 8:22ff. that wisdom was with God from all eternity. Before the universe was brought into existence wisdom was there. Identified as a preexistent "master workman," wisdom appears as the creative agent through whom the universe was fashioned. In the Proverbs passage wisdom is more than the personification of a divine attribute. The coeternal creative workman is a distinct foreshadowing of Jesus Christ, "the wisdom of God" (1 Cor. 2:7, KJV; see Col. 2:3).

Isaiah 9:6 is a clear prophecy of Israel's Messiah. Whereas the prophet earlier focused on the uniqueness of the Messiah's birth (7:14) here he stresses the marvel of His character. The Messiah is described by the titles "Wonderful Counselor" (lit. "Supernatural Counselor") and "Mighty God." In addition, He is the "Eternal Father," or in the original, "the Father of Eternity." It was the custom of the Jews to call a person who possessed a thing the "father" of it. A wise man was then "the father of wisdom." "Father of Eternity," therefore, indicates that the Messiah is the possessor of eternity.

The prophet Micah spoke even more plainly to the issue. The babe who would be born in obscure Bethlehem is one "whose origin is from old, from ancient days" (Micah 5:2, RSV). The Messiah clearly preexisted His birth of the virgin Mary.

New Testament Development

Liberal Protestants frequently claim that Jesus was neither conscious of nor claimed to be God's preexistent Son. True, Jesus exercised restraint in speaking of His prior existence with the Father. It was never the Lord's habit to satisfy the idle curiosity of the onlooker. The proclamation of Jesus' preexistence by the Church had to await the accomplishment of His atoning work and resurrection from the dead.

The Gospels make clear, however, that our Lord was aware of His heavenly origin. In talking with a Pharisee named Nicodemus, Jesus spoke with authority about the things of God because of His heavenly origin (John 3:13, 31). Later, after Jesus had miraculously fed the 5,000, the crowd eagerly followed Him with hopes of further handouts. Jesus responded by referring to Himself as "the manna," the bread of the new life (John 6:22-59).

The Jews of Jesus' day believed that when the Messiah came He would again supply Israel with manna. So the Jewish leaders challenged Jesus to prove He was the Messiah by producing the heavenly manna. Jesus then astounded the Jews by claiming seven times that He was the living manna which had come down from heaven. He, on whom all mankind depends for spiritual existence, was eternally existent.

Later, during His final hours with the twelve disciples prior to the cross, Jesus indicated in plain terms that just as He had come from the Father, so He would shortly leave the world for a heavenly reunion (John 16:27-28).

One of the greatest claims Jesus made is recorded by Matthew: "All things have been handed over to Me by My Father; and no one knows the Son except the Father, nor does anyone know the Father, except the Son" (Matt. 11:27, NASB). This profound knowledge of the Father that Jesus claimed could hardly have been gained during His short lifetime. That is why Alfred Plummer, in his commentary on Matthew, says that the word "delivered" is timeless and "points back to a moment in eternity, and implies the preexistence of the Messiah."

The character, teaching, and deeds of Jesus were such that others caught a glimpse of His timelessness. John the Baptist said, "After me comes a Man who has a higher rank than I, for He existed before me" (John 1:30). After the raising of Lazarus from the tomb, Martha recognized Jesus as the promised Christ who was to visit the world (11:27). And following the feeding of the 5,000 many people recognized the sign and acknowledged Jesus as the Prophet who came from God (6:14).

John, Paul, and the writer of the Book of Hebrews show the greatest interest in Christ's preexistence. The Prologue of the fourth Gospel (1:1-18) contains by far the fullest description of what Calvin calls "the eternal divinity of Christ." John identifies Jesus by the title "Word," in Greek *Logos*. "Word" was a concept full of meaning in both Greek and Hebrew thought. To a Greek *Logos* was the creating and guiding power of God. Without the *Logos* the universe would make no sense. To the Jewish mind *Logos* signified the living expression or communication of Jehovah. Endowed with an existence which is dynamic and powerful, the

Word was God clothed with creative power (Ps. 33:6; Isa. 55:11; Jer. 23:29). In short, for John the Word was a roundabout way of speaking of God.

In the first verse of his Gospel John makes three profound statements about the Word. Each of these declarations carries us back to the distant reaches of eternity. The first focuses on His *eternal subsistence*: "In the beginning the Word was." John leads the reader back to Genesis 1:1 and to the absolute beginning of time and creation. The sun, moon, and stars "came into being" through Him (John 1:3), but the Word in the beginning "was." He shared in an "absolute, supratemporal existence." He was always there, before the beginning of things. The *Logos* is part of eternity.

Second, John focuses on his *eternal communion* with God: "the Word was with God." When nothing but God had being, the Word was there in closest relation to the Father. Alexander Maclaren, the influential preacher at the turn of the 20th century, notes that the other Gospels begin with Bethlehem. John, however, begins with the heart of the Father.

Finally, John stresses the Logos' *eternal identity* with God: "and the Word was God." John wants us to know that the Word was not merely God's eternal companion; He was in truth God Himself. In personal subsistence, communion with God and identity, the Son is truly eternal.

In another vivid image John portrays Jesus as "the first and the last" (Rev. 1:17; 2:8), then as "the Alpha and the Omega, the beginning and the end" (Rev. 21:6), and finally, heaping phrase upon phrase, he describes Jesus as "the Alpha and the Omega, the first and the last, the beginning and the end" (Rev. 22:13). Alpha and Omega are the first and last letters of the Greek alphabet. They indicate, according to John, that Christ is the beginning, the means, and the end of all things.

Paul's most explicit passage dealing with Christ's preexistence is Philippians 2:5-11. Here the Apostle urges the Philippians to imitate Christ's example of humility. Christ didn't rely on some heavenly passport as protection against loss of status and privilege. What was His by right He was willing to forego for the good of others. From eternity Christ possessed the form of God Himself. But moved by love, He refused His rights and took the form of a lowly servant. The Lord exchanged the riches of eternity for the rebuke of time. P. T. Forsyth, the English theologian, once said, "Unlike us, He chose the oblivion of birth and the humiliation of life. He consented not only to die, but to be born."

We find a final remarkable portrait of the Son of God in the Book of Hebrews. In the seventh chapter of Hebrews Christ is represented in terms of Melchizedek, the ancient priest-king of Salem (Gen. 14:18ff.). This mysterious figure out of Genesis is a type of Christ in that he was "without father, without mother, without genealogy, having neither beginning of days nor end of life" (Heb. 7:3). These words apply to Melchizedek symbolically, in that details of his life are not recorded in Scripture. But they are true of Christ actually, in the sense that He possesses neither beginning nor end of personal existence. He is the timelessly eternal one. He is "Jesus Christ . . . the same yesterday and today, yes and forever" (Heb. 13:8).

Scientists inform us that we humans are constantly changing. The molecules of our physical bodies die and are replaced every few years. Someone said, "Our little systems have their day; they have their day and cease to be." But amidst the flux of the created world stands our eternal and unchanging Saviour. "They will . . . be changed. But Thou art the same" (Heb. 1:12).

How Far Preexistent?

We can draw together now the lines of truth we have considered in this chapter. We have noted that Jesus' birth at Bethlehem did not mark the beginning of His existence. Of no other person in history was this ever true. Caesar, Napoleon, and Churchill had their origins in the normal cycle of conception and birth. But Jesus Christ differed radically from these great men. As we search behind Bethlehem to our Lord's beginnings we embark on a fascinating journey.

The Bible is clear that Christ existed before His birth. The later prophets in Israel envisioned the Son as the Shekinah glory (the "dwelling of God") descending upon the temple and the holy city

(Ezek. 11:23; 43:2; see also Rev. 1:13-15). Whenever we find the Shekinah glory in the Old Testament, the Lord Christ was there. At the time of Daniel, for example, three young men were thrown by Nebuchadnezzar into a roaring furnace. In the midst of the glowing fire a fourth man was seen, whose appearance was like that of the Son of God (Dan. 3:24-25).

Earlier, in David's day, a full millennium before the first Christmas, the son of Jesse could say: "The Lord says to my Lord: 'Sit at My right hand, till I make Your enemies Your footstool'" (Ps. 110:1, RSV). The Psalm is referring to Christ, David's Lord. We know this because Jesus Himself used it in this way, to suggest His own deity (Matt. 22:41-46).

Back still further in Old Testament history, during the conquest of Canaan, Joshua encountered a man with a drawn sword in his hand. The Bible identifies the stranger as the Captain of the Lord's host—likely an appearance of the Son of God in human form (Josh. 5:13-15). Earlier still, during Israel's wilderness wanderings, God provided water through the rock smitten by Moses (Ex. 17:6). Inspired by the Spirit, Paul claimed that "the rock was Christ" (1 Cor. 10:4). Back in Abraham's day three men appeared at the door of the patriarch's tent, one of whom may have been the preincarnate Word (Gen. 18:2ff.).

Finally, thousands of years earlier, at Creation, the Christ was present. As John, Paul, and the writer to the Hebrews explain, the Son was the agent through whom the entire universe was brought into existence. Scripture, then, drives us back to eternity past where we find the Christ existing with the Father in the triune Godhead. Multiplying water drops by grains of sand we grope to fathom the vision of the psalmist who wrote, "Before the mountains were brought forth, or ever Thou hadst formed the earth and the world, even from everlasting to everlasting, Thou art God" (Ps. 90:2, KJV).

How, then, shall we conceive of the preexistence of our Lord? Someone has said, "It is duration without beginning or end, existence without bound or dimension, present without past or future, youth without infancy or old age, life without birth or death, and today without yesterday or tomorrow."

3

"God of God"

Jesus Christ is the foundation of the Christian faith (1 Cor. 3:11). Christianity rests upon the uniqueness, indeed the deity, of Jesus of Nazareth. Accept this basic doctrine of Scripture and the entire Christian scheme of incarnation, miracles, atonement, and resurrection makes supremely good sense. Abandon this central fact and the faith collapses into confusion.

Christians may differ on the mode of baptism, on the role of women in the church, or on the fine points of prophecy. But true Christians, whatever their denomination, agree that everything turns on the deity of Christ.

Let's examine more closely the Christian claim that Jesus was God. The designation, Jesus Christ, combines a name and a title. The name Jesus is the Greek form of *Jeshua,* meaning "Jehovah-Saviour" or "the Lord saves" (Isa. 43:3). The title Christ is the Greek form of the Hebrew *Mashiach,* which means "anointed one" (Dan. 9:26) or Messiah. *Jesus Christ,* therefore, signifies the special messianic Saviour promised by the Old Testament.

Scripture teaches that Jesus was endowed with the nature and attributes of God Himself. Some Christians, however, prefer to speak of Jesus' "divinity." How does this term differ from "deity"? Traditionally, "deity" and "divinity" were used interchangeably. Both meant the same thing. But in modern times liberal Protestants have weakened the term *divinity* by defining it in the metaphorical sense of "what is sacred or religious." For this reason evangelical Christians prefer to speak of the deity rather than the divinity of Christ.

A famous New York preacher once discussed the question of Jesus' relation to God. "All will agree," he said, "that Jesus was an extraordinary person—an individual superior to other men in spiritual insight and devotion. We may accept Jesus' teachings as the basis of our faith. But to claim that the carpenter of Nazareth is the Creator God of the universe is sheer superstition."

A responsible view of Jesus Christ, however, rests not on human opinion or on the current philosophical fad, but on the express teaching of Holy Scripture. Our attitude to Him is derived solely from the Word of God. Two prominent students of the New Testament put it this way:

The belief in the deity of Christ is derived directly from statements concerning Him in the Bible. The references are so many and their meaning so plain that Christians of every shade of opinion have always regarded its affirmation as an absolute and indispensable requisite of their faith. It is proclaimed in the very first sermon of the infant church (Acts 2:36) . . .; while in the last vision of the Book of Revelation the Lamb occupying *one* throne with God (Rev. 22:3) can betoken only essential oneness (F. F. Bruce, and W. J. Martin, "The Deity of Christ," *Christianity Today* IX.6, Dec. 18, 1964, p.11).

It proves helpful to arrange the biblical evidence for Christ's deity under four main headings: Christ's Names, Qualities, Works, and Claims.

Godlike Names
The names which the New Testament applies to Christ lead to only one conclusion: Jesus Christ was accepted by early believers as a divine person. In all, some 16 such titles are recorded in the New Testament. Limitations of space dictate that we discuss only the most prominent of these.

The most compelling proof of Christ's deity is His designation as "God." With simple directness John says of Christ, "the Word was God" (John 1:1). The absence of the article before "God" focuses attention on Christ's nature. The *New English Bible* puts it well: "What God was, the Word was."

A bit later in the same passage (John 1:18) John makes a similar statement. Although some authorities read "Son" in this verse, the evidence is strong for the reading adopted by the *New American Standard Bible,* which refers to Jesus as "the only begotten God, who is in the bosom of the Father." Later in the fourth Gospel Thomas is so convinced of Jesus' deity that he acknowledges the risen Christ as, "My Lord and my God!" (John 20:28)

Paul, too, addressed Jesus directly as God. To Titus he spoke of Christ as "our great God and Saviour" (Titus 2:13). And Romans 9:5 refers to Him as "God blessed forever." In a similar way the anonymous writer of Hebrews applies Psalm 45:6 to Jesus as proof of His deity: "Thy throne, O God, is forever and ever" (Heb. 1:8). It is clear, then, that Jesus was designated "God" in the New Testament.

The Bible also knows Jesus as the "Son of God." Our Lord used the title of Himself only infrequently, but others applied it to Him on many occasions. Son of God was a familiar title in Jewish circles. Angels (Job 38:7), magistrates (Ps. 82:6-7), kings (Ps. 89:26-27), the nation Israel (Ex. 4:22), and the Messiah (Ps. 2:7) were all called sons of God. In the New Testament Adam (Luke 3:38) and Christian believers (1 John 3:1) are designated by the same phrase.

To the Jewish mind "son of God" implied a very special relation with Yahweh. But in Jesus' case, this relationship was absolutely unique. He was one with the Father in the eternal Godhead. Peter recognized this (Matt. 16:16), and Caiaphas pondered it (Matt. 26:63-65).

Jesus' sonship is most prominent, however, in John's Gospel. In this Gospel, Jesus regards God as His Father (5:18) and openly claims to be God's Son (10:33, 36). For the Jews this was tantamount to blasphemy and deserved only death (19:6-7).

Several times John calls Jesus the "only begotten Son" of God (1:14, 18; 3:16, 18). Literally, the title means "only one of its kind" or "unique." "Only begotten Son" plainly distinguishes

Christ from God's other "sons." Christ is in a class by Himself, in that His personhood came forth from the essence of the Father. Significantly, the New Testament also applies to Jesus the name and title, "Lord." Nearly 250 times, in fact. To be sure, "Lord" is often used as a courtesy title in the sense of sir, master, or owner. The Roman emperor, for example, adopted the title and demanded worship from his subjects. When applied to Jesus, however, "Lord" is the New Testament equivalent of *Yahweh* and *Adonai* in the Old Testament. In Matthew 3:3, for example, John the Baptist cites Isaiah 40:3 and applies the words directly to Jesus: "Make ready the way of the Lord, make His paths straight!" Lord, then, is an obvious title of deity. It signifies that Christ is the divine ruler over God's kingdom.

Another of Jesus' titles is "Lord of Glory." Paul observes the supreme injustice, that the rulers of this world crucified the Lord of glory (1 Cor. 2:8). When he used this title, the Apostle undoubtedly had in mind the ringing chorus of Psalm 24:7-10, where Yahweh is depicted as "the King of glory, . . . the Lord strong and mighty."

Jesus is also represented as "the Holy One" (Acts 3:14). We may recall that "Holy One" was a common Old Testament name for Israel's God. The prophet Isaiah used the title some 30 times (e.g., Isa. 30:15) of Yahweh.

From such a brief survey of some New Testament titles for Jesus the conclusion is inescapable that our Lord was called God. Anyone who honestly assesses the evidence will be compelled to say with Daniel Webster, "I believe Jesus Christ to be the Son of God."

Godlike Qualities

Few people who have seriously read the Gospels have not been deeply impressed by the character of Jesus. Who embodies more fully than Jesus the moral and spiritual values which make up true greatness?

During the turbulent '60s, students at a California university protested against the "establishment." One carried a sign which read, "Jesus Christ, *Yes*—Christianity, *No*." Hostility against organized Christendom could not quench a deep fascination for the person of Jesus. No wonder then that Jesus remains the most attractive and popular figure in the world's history. Ralph Waldo Emerson was absolutely right when he declared that "Jesus is the most perfect of all men that have yet appeared."

One of Jesus' remarkable claims is recorded in John 16:15: "All things that the Father has are mine." Here Jesus insisted that He possesses the attributes, or characteristics and qualities of God Himself. If Jesus actually possesses the divine attributes, then we would have further evidence of His true deity.

Theologians divide the attributes or qualities of God in two categories, known as moral and metaphysical. The moral attributes are those which are shared by Creator and creature alike: love, holiness, truth, and the like. The difference is that in God those qualities are present in absolute perfection.

The metaphysical attributes, however, God shares with no one. His self-existence, infinity, omnipotence, and so on, are not communicable. It follows that if these attributes which are not shared with any creature are present in Christ, then He must be God Himself. Let's first consider these attributes.

Logically the first metaphysical attribute of God is *self-existence*. This perfection implies that the source of God's life is in Himself. His existence depends on nothing outside His own being.

John assigns this foremost attribute of deity to Jesus. In John 1:4 we read "in Him was life." Later in this Gospel our Lord Himself claimed, "I am the life" (14:6). Notice that Jesus did not say "I have life," but "I am life." Peter caught the difference, for in an early sermon he rebuked the Jews for killing "the Author of life" (Acts 3:15, NIV). Clearly the apostles regarded Jesus as the self-existent "I AM."

Since we considered Christ's *eternity* in chapter 2, we can move on here to consider how the Gospels portray Jesus as *omniscient* (or all-knowing). He knew the thoughts of the Samaritan woman (John 4:16ff.), perceived the reasonings of the scribes and Pharisees (Luke 5:21ff.), and penetrated the whisperings of the tax collectors (Matt. 17:24ff.). In truth, Jesus knew all men (John 2:25). The fact that He "increased in wisdom and stature"

(Luke 2:52, KJV) is simply part of the mystery of the God who was also man.

Jesus Himself made the bold claim that He was *omnipotent* or all-mighty (John 5:19). Evidences in the Gospels of His omnipotence are legion. Consider His supreme power over disease (Luke 4:39), death (Luke 7:12ff.), nature (Matt. 8:24ff.), and the destiny of His own life as man (John 10:18).

Finally, Jesus is *incomprehensible*. Finite man cannot plumb the depths of His being (Matt. 11:27; Eph. 3:8). In this life, our knowledge of Christ, though true, is always only partial.

From the New Testament we may likewise conclude that the moral attributes or qualities of God were also perfectly embodied in Jesus Christ. In a bold statement which includes moral excellencies, Paul testifies that "in Him all the fullness of deity dwells" (Col. 2:9). Inspired Scripture tells us that Christ is *holy* (Luke 1:35; Acts 3:14), *true* (John 14:6; Rev. 3:7), *loving* (Eph. 3:19; 1 John 3:16), *faithful* (Rev. 3:14; 19:11), and *merciful* (James 5:11; Jude 21). Jesus' moral perfection is at the heart of His continuing appeal to people of every generation. Ultimately, it furnishes further proof of His claim to deity.

The facts which emerge as we consider Christ's qualities or attributes force us to agree with Horace Bushnell who said, "The character of Jesus Christ forbids His possible classification with men."

Godlike Works

Even the casual reader of the New Testament will admit that works are attributed to Christ which are properly works of God alone. Jesus appears to have been aware of the divine character of His deeds. After healing a blind man Jesus exclaimed, "I must work the works of Him that sent me" (John 9:4, KJV). No mere man ever claimed to perform the cosmic works which the Bible attributes to Christ.

Scripture makes the awesome claim that Christ played a part in the creation of the universe. In the Bible Creation is first and foremost a work of God (Pss. 95; 104; Rev. 4:11). Yet the New Testament claims that Christ is the creative agent of the universe.

For John (John 1:3), Paul (Col. 1:16), and the writer of Hebrews (Heb. 1:2), all that is—God alone excepted—was created by the Son.

President Theodore Roosevelt was fascinated with the sheer vastness of the universe. On a cloudless night he would point out to visitors the small cluster of stars called Andromeda. Then Roosevelt would remark that Andromeda was as large as the Milky Way galaxy. It is 770,000 light years distant and consists of 100 billion suns, each larger than our sun. Yet Andromeda, like the Milky Way, is but one of 100 million galaxies in the universe!

The human mind bogs down before the vastness of the universe. Yet the Bible insists that Christ the Son brought it all into being.

Christ, this author of Creation, is also, so the Bible teaches, the agent of preservation. He holds it all together. Scripture rarely speaks of our Lord's creative work without mentioning His sustaining activity (Col. 1:16-17; Heb. 1:2-3). Paul made a particularly striking statement to the Colossians: "In Him all things hold together" (Col. 1:17). The English phrase *hold together* means in Greek "to piece together" or "to cohere." The idea is that of an interlocking jigsaw puzzle where all the pieces perfectly fit and grip each other in place. The Apostle claims that Jesus Christ is the "interlocker" in the vast and intricate jigsaw of the universe.

Apart from Christ the universe would disintegrate. Without His preserving power the cosmos would instantly become a chaos. A. H. Strong, the Baptist theologian, claimed that "the laws of nature are the habits of Christ." And the great scientist Isaac Newton insisted that the force of gravity is an expression of the mind of Christ.

A further mark which attests Christ's deity is His direction and control of the course of history. Paul saw Christ at the center of Israel's growth from a people in Egyptian bondage to a nation established in the land (1 Cor. 10:1-11). In Revelation it is the lamb who opens the seven seals, thus ordering the events which will consummate the present age (Rev. 5:5; 6:1, 3, 5). A famous French philosopher touched on an element of the truth when he claimed that Christ is the "Omega"—the goal to which human history and the universe tend.

The ancient Greeks saw no purpose or end to the historical process. History ebbed and flowed in a random cyclic pattern. Many modern thinkers endorse this Greek view of history. One typical European theologian says that we cannot claim to know the end and goal of history. The question of meaning in history itself has become meaningless. But behind all the events reported in our newspapers and TV sets is poised the providential hand of Jesus Christ. World events are working out according to His plan.

In addition to Christ's work in the universe, however, the Bible teaches that He has power to forgive sins. During His ministry Jesus demonstrated His authority when He forgave the sins of a paralytic (Mark 2:3ff.). The Jewish scribes recognized the implications of this and charged our Lord with blasphemy. "Who can forgive sins but God alone?" they exclaimed.

Christ performed a similar work of God when He raised Lazarus from the dead (John 11:17ff.). The raising of Lazarus was an early example of Christ's work of raising the dead in the last day (John 11:25-26). That is how John and other early Christians came to see it. Only one who is equal with God, the Gospel says, could perform such a mighty work (John 5:21).

Related to this is the equally stupendous fact that Christ will judge all men. Jesus taught that "the Father judges no one, but has given all judgment to the Son" (John 5:22; see also v. 27). Thus at the close of the age Christ will execute judgment on all men—"the living and the dead" (Acts 10:42; 2 Tim. 4:1), the nations of earth (Acts 17:31), and the forces of Antichrist (Rev. 19:15ff.). None but an all wise, all just God could perform such a work.

Taken together, the works attributed to Christ offer convincing proof of His authentic Godhead. The story is told of a Japanese student who wanted to learn English. After a while he was given the Gospel of John to work through. Upon reading of Jesus' works he became very restless. "Who is this Jesus about whom I have been reading?" he asked. "You call Him a man, but He must be God."

Godlike Claims

Further evidence of Christ's deity is found in the astonishing claims He made. True, anyone can make claims about himself. But the claims Christ made cannot be lightly disregarded. Christ claimed to enjoy the closest possible relation to God. Consequently, to know Him is to know God (John 8:19; 14:7). To see Him is to see God (John 12:45; 14:9). To receive Him is to receive God (Mark 9:37). And to honor Him is to honor God (John 5:23). All this is true, because Jesus said, "I and the Father are one" (John 10:30). The Jews rightly interpreted this saying as a claim to deity. And for such blasphemy they sought to kill Jesus.

In addition, Jesus claimed to be the object of saving faith, on equal terms with the Father. He urged people to believe on Him as they believe on the Father (John 14:1). He promised eternal life to those who know the Father and Jesus Christ His Son (John 17:3).

Yet Christ frequently upheld Himself as the sole object of faith and devotion. Thus our Lord said, "Come unto Me" (Matt. 11:28), "Believe on Me" (John 3:36), "Follow Me" (Matt. 4:19), "Love Me" (John 14:15), and "Do this in remembrance of Me" (1 Cor. 11:24-25).

It is clear that Christ also claimed absolute dominion over His followers. They were to leave all and follow Him as their captain and king. In Scripture the family is upheld as a divinely ordained institution (Matt. 19:4-6). Yet if a conflict of loyalty should arise, ultimate allegiance is due to Jesus (Matt. 10:37-39). There is no hint in the Bible that Christ's claims to Lordship were anything but fully justified. He is Lord of all!

Moreover, Christ claimed sovereignty over the laws and institutions of God. God gave the Law through Moses, whom Israel held in highest esteem. Yet Christ claimed to give a new interpretation and a deeper meaning to the revered Law (Matt. 5:21ff.). Similarly, Christ claimed jurisdiction over the Covenant (Matt. 26:28), the Sabbath (Matt. 12:8), the temple (Matt. 12:6), and indeed, the kingdom of God itself (Matt. 16:19).

Finally, we observe that Christ received the honor and worship due to God alone. Christ taught that only the God of heaven is to be worshiped (Matt. 4:10). Yet Thomas worshiped Christ as he would God (John 20:28). So did Stephen (Acts 7:59), the disciples (Matt. 14:33), and the angels of heaven (Heb. 1:6). Indeed, one day the entire universe will bow in homage before Him (Phil. 2:10-11).

The conclusion is inescapable that Jesus made awesome claims for Himself. William Biederwolf, a popular preacher of yesteryear, put it this way: "A man who can read the New Testament and not see that Christ claims to be more than a man, can look all over the sky at high noon on a cloudless day and not see the sun."

But how seriously can we take these claims? Someone has said that more than 2,000 people in our generation alone claim to be the Messiah. Many of these are undoubtedly insane. But what about Jesus? Can His claims to deity be taken seriously? In his book *Mere Christianity,* C. S. Lewis surely has spoken the final word on this matter. Writes Lewis,

A man who was merely a man and said the sort of things Jesus said wouldn't be a great moral teacher. He would either be a lunatic—on a level with a man who says he is a poached egg—or else he'd be the devil of hell. You must make your choice. Either this man was, and is, the Son of God, or else a madman or something worse (*Mere Christianity,* Fontana Books, 1952, p. 52).

When it comes to Jesus' claims to deity we are dealing with a case of "either-or." Either Jesus is the Christ He claimed to be, or He was an imposter and a blasphemer. But if Jesus was a blasphemer, Christians for nearly 2,000 years have been idolaters. But this cannot be. For a knave could not have captured the hearts and minds of so great a company down through the years as Jesus has done.

In summary, then, Jesus' names, qualities, works, and claims, as well as the faith experience of His people, confirm the Godhead of our Lord Jesus Christ.

The Christian claim that Jesus Christ is the true God is neither superstitious nor sentimental. If Jesus were not God the church would have no supernatural Saviour who could atone for sins. We sinners then would be consigned to our guilt and misery forever. Martin Luther expressed this truth beautifully.

If Christ does not remain true, natural God . . . then we are lost. For what good would the suffering and death of the Lord Christ do me if He were merely a man such as you and I are? Then He would not have been able to overcome the devil, death, and sin. He would have been far too weak for them and could not have helped us (*Luthers Werke,* Weimer Edition, Vol. 46, p. 554).

If Jesus were not the Christ of God, the church erected on His foundation would collapse and be buried in the sands of time. As the poet Carlyle put it, "Had this doctrine of the divinity of Christ been lost, Christianity would have vanished like a dream."

4

God Become Man

After the first American astronaut landed on the moon, the president of the United States praised this wonder of modern science. "The planting of human feet on the moon," he said, "is the greatest moment in human history."

Later evangelist Billy Graham set matters straight. "With all due respect," he said, "the greatest moment in human history was not when man set foot on the moon, but when the infinite and eternal God set foot on the earth in Jesus of Nazareth." The president had the enthusiasm; but the evangelist knew the truth.

The incarnation of God in Jesus is what life on Planet Earth is all about. The Almighty God entered the human scene at Bethlehem in the form of Mary's child. The Babe cradled in that cow stall was the God of creation manifested in the helplessness of an infant's life. He came in weakness in order that we might find God's power. Think of it as the story of a king who left his throne and identified with his rebellious subjects to restore them to his kingdom. "Christianity," as C. S. Lewis put it, "is the story of how the rightful king has landed, you might say landed in disguise."

That invasion of our planet is a cardinal doctrine of the Christian faith. As Martin Luther noted, "After the article of the Trinity the one of the incarnation of the Son of God is the sublimest."

By the Incarnation we mean that the eternal Son of God took to Himself a genuine human nature and lived a genuine human life on earth without for a moment ceasing to be deity.

The term "incarnation" (from the Latin, "in flesh") is not a biblical word. The idea, however, is thoroughly biblical. John put it simply when he wrote: "Jesus Christ has come in the flesh" (1 John 4:2; see also 2 John 7). Perhaps his most moving lines, however, are found in John 1:14: "The Word became flesh and dwelt among us, full of grace and truth; we have beheld His glory, glory as of the only Son from the Father" (RSV).

Luther, who often told a story in order to make a point, stressed the impact of God assuming flesh when he described a preacher reading from the first chapter of John's Gospel. When he came to the words, "In the beginning was the Word," the devil stood motionless. But when he read, "and the Word was made flesh," he immediately fled.

John's Prologue (John 1:1-18) teaches four important truths about the Incarnation: First, John points to the *subject* of the Incarnation: the eternally divine *Logos* or Word of God. "In the beginning was the Word" (John 1:1).

Next, he unfolds the *substance* of the Incarnation: "the Word became flesh" (John 1:14). The language suggests that the Word experienced a change of state more profound than a mere birth. "Flesh" in Scripture is used in two main ways. On the one hand, it denotes the seat of sin in man (John 3:6; Rom. 8:3). But on the other, as here, John used "flesh" in the sense of human nature in general without moral disparagement (see also John 1:13; 1 Cor. 15:39). By saying that the eternal Word came in "flesh," John teaches that the *Logos* assumed complete humanity, sin excepted.

Third, John identifies the *scene* of the Incarnation: the eternal *Logos* "dwelt among us." The word "dwelt," in the original, means to pitch a temporary tent or tabernacle. At His incarnation the Son tabernacled in the tent of our humanity, much as God dwelt with His people of old in the early tabernacle (2 Sam. 7:6).

Finally, John records the *substantiation* of the Incarnation: "we beheld His glory." God's visitation of earth was no secret operation staged in a maximum security zone. For three years the disciples witnessed heaven's invasion of earth through the man Jesus.

S. D. Gordon, who wrote so many moving lines of devotion, summarized John 1:14 in one striking sentence: "Jesus is God spelling Himself out in language that men can understand."

Biblical Symbolism for the Incarnation

In his teaching about the Incarnation the Apostle John offered no explanation of *how* the eternal God took to Himself complete humanity. There is a reason for that. Paul said, "By common confession great is the mystery of godliness: He who was revealed in the flesh, was vindicated in the Spirit" (1 Tim. 3:16). The fact is that the incarnation of God in Christ is a mystery too profound for the human mind to fully grasp. The Christian, nevertheless, accepts by faith Scripture's testimony to this awesome event.

From the language they used, however, we can gain from the New Testament writers some insight into the character of this profound mystery. The Synoptic Gospels (Matt., Mark, and Luke) tell us that the Son of man came to serve (Matt. 20:28); Jesus' coming to earth was a voluntary act. According to John, Jesus frequently spoke of Himself as one who "descended" (John 3:13), or "came down from heaven" (John 6:41, 51); Jesus' ascent was preceded by a single descent. Similarly, Jesus is one "whom God has sent" into the world on a special mission (John 3:34; see also John 4:34; 5:36).

Paul builds on John's language when he refers to God's *"sending* His own Son in the likeness of sinful flesh" (Rom. 8:3). The initiative, Paul stresses, lies with God the Father. And for an interesting reason. Second Corinthians 8:9 reads, "though He was rich, yet . . . He became poor"; the Son, rich from eternity, became incredibly poor in time. Then, Paul adds, "when the fullness of time came, God sent forth His Son, born of a woman" (Gal. 4:4); the Son who was dispatched on an earthly mission derived His humanity from Mary.

The classic Pauline passage on the Incarnation, however, is Philippians 2:6-8. Although Christ subsisted in the form of God,

He didn't selfishly cling to His status of equality with God. The insignia of deity—the glory and the majesty of God—He was willing to lay aside. Thus He "emptied Himself, taking the form of a bond servant and being made in the likeness of men." Paul does not suggest that the eternal *Logos* exchanged His deity for humanity. Although from an outward appearance He became authentically man, he never ceased to be fully God.

Finally, we find the unusual stress on the humanity of our Lord in the Book of Hebrews. Chapter two describes the dynamics of the Incarnation. The writer explains that "[Jesus] was made for a little while lower than the angels" (2:9). Moreover, Jesus and those He came to save "are all of one stock" (2:11, NEB). He took to Himself our "flesh and blood" through the process of a human birth (2:14), and identified with a particular segment of the human family, namely, the descendants of Abraham (2:16). The Lord was born a Jew. This solidarity with the human race was necessary in order to cleanse our sins and serve as a true high priest. Hence we read that Jesus "had to be made like His brethren in all things" (2:17).

The news media inform us that UFO sightings have increased in recent years. An official government report on the problem indicates, however, that no firm evidence exists that anyone from outer space has ever visited our planet. The eye of faith must differ with this judgment. Earth has been visited from "outer space." The incarnate Christ from glory has come. That is the greatest event in human history.

"With the Incarnation came the Man," says the English journalist Malcolm Muggeridge, "and the addition of a new spiritual dimension to the cosmic scene. The universe provides a stage; Jesus is the play."

Incarnation and Manhood

We have shown how Scripture plainly teaches that in Christ God became a real man. We are left, however, with a question, one the disciples raised after Jesus had stilled the storm on the sea, "What kind of man is this?" (Matt. 8:27) Jesus was patently a man, but what sort of man? The uniqueness of Jesus' humanity prompted Pontius Pilate to cry out to the mob, "Behold, the Man!" (John 19:5)

It comes as no surprise that enemies of the Christian faith have challenged our Lord's deity. But it is no less true that our Saviour's humanity has come under attack. Some early Eastern movements held that matter was inherently evil. God could contact the material world only through a chain of intermediary beings. Influenced by this type of thinking, a group called the Docetists claimed that Christ came only in the appearance of flesh. Significantly, the earliest heresy was a denial not of Christ's Godhead but of His Manhood. John wrote his first letter to counter this false teaching (1 John 1:1; 4:2).

Later, in the fourth century, followers of Apollinarius, the bishop of Laodicea, argued that Jesus was an incomplete man. At the incarnation Jesus' rational soul was replaced by the heavenly *Logos*. In the modern world some sects perpetuate these old heresies. Mary Baker Eddy, for example, denied Jesus' real humanity by teaching that "Christ is incorporeal and spiritual."

The best answer to false views, old and new, is the portrait of Jesus in the Gospels, sketched by men who knew Him best. Whatever difficulties the Virgin Birth presents, or the relationship of Christ's humanity and deity, one fact is certain: Jesus was an authentic man. In the Gospels Jesus' ancestry is traced back to Abraham (Matt. 1:1) and beyond that to Adam (Luke 3:38). Like us He had a mother (Gal. 4:4) who brought Him into the world (Luke 2:7). As a youth Jesus grew up normally (Luke 2:40, 52) in a family which included four "brothers" and at least two "sisters." Like other men He worked with His hands at a carpenter's bench (Mark 6:3).

From the Gospels we also learn that Jesus had a real, physical body. He experienced hunger (Luke 4:2), thirst (John 19:28), weariness (John 4:6), temptation (Matt. 4:1), anger (John 2:15ff.)—in short, the whole range of human infirmities (Heb. 5:2). He ate and drank (Luke 7:34), wept (John 11:35), slept (Matt. 8:24), prayed (Luke 5:16), and loved His family and friends (John 11:3; 19:26). When Jesus faced the end He felt deep sorrow and anxiety (Mark 14:34). On the cross He died a

cruel and agonizing death (Matt. 27:46, 50). With the prophet
we behold Jesus, "a man of sorrows, and acquainted with grief"
(Isa. 53:3).

Certainly, Jesus was fully conscious of His manhood. The Bible
recognizes body, soul, and spirit as the three functional elements
of human nature. Jesus spoke of the reality of His body (Matt.
26:12), of His soul (Matt. 26:38), and of His spirit (Luke
23:46). The records throughout testify that Jesus was a man no
less human than we.

But Jesus differed from us in one significant respect; His manhood was untainted by the corruption of sin. He who called others
to repentance had no need to seek forgiveness for any sin of His
own for He embodied the highest, holiest manhood the world
has ever known.

Today's newspapers are filled with reports of people demanding human rights. The fact is that mankind in its fallen state is
subhuman. In character and conduct man is a pale image of the
original, unspoiled creation of God. Only in Jesus do we see
authentic, uncorrupted humanity as God intended it.

The Renunciation of the Incarnation

The classic Pauline text affirming the Incarnation is, as we have
noted, Philippians 2:6-8. Here Paul stated that although the
Christ existed in a state of equality with God, He willingly "emptied Himself" assuming the form of a servant. Out of this passage
has emerged the so-called "kenosis" or "self-emptying" theory of
the Incarnation.

In the 19th century, liberal Protestants thought only of the
human Jesus who walked the dusty paths of Palestine. Many held
that a Jesus who possessed all glory, knowledge, and power could
not be a real man like us. So they reinterpreted the Incarnation.
When the *Logos* became a man, they said, He divested Himself
of deity. Whereas Christ retained His moral perfections of love,
holiness, justice, etc., He laid aside His metaphysical perfections
of omniscience, omnipresence, and omnipotence. The "kenosis"
theory thus meant the transformation of God into a man.

The evangelical Christian must reject such a view of the "kenosis" because it flatly compromises Christ's deity. At the Incarnation Christ laid aside, not His deity, but the voluntary exercise of some of His Divine powers. When He came to earth, our Lord surrendered the use of His divine attributes of omniscience, omnipresence, and omnipotence. Thus He not only wept and grew weary, but He was ignorant of matters one would expect God to know (Matt. 24:36). Jesus could have retained all knowledge. He could have known the very hour of His return in glory. He could have come down from the cross and destroyed His enemies. But He did none of these because He freely accepted the limitations of our humanity.

This limitation of divine attributes is evident in the fact that Jesus developed intellectually, physically, spiritually, and socially (Luke 2:52). "He learned obedience from the things which He suffered" (Heb. 5:8). In a famous essay on the Incarnation, *Why God Became Man,* Anselm, the medieval Christian philosopher, found the developing manhood of Jesus a difficult doctrine. "It is said," he wrote, "that our Lord increased in wisdom and in favor with God. This was not really the case; Jesus merely deported Himself as if it were so." On Anselm's view, Jesus' growth into manhood was imaginary, not real. Anselm thus reflected the thought of his time, for by medieval times Jesus had become a kind of Greek god of mythology who descended to earth fully grown.

A similar view is in "The Gospel of Infancy," one of the spurious, apocryphal gospels. We read there that several small boys interrupted the young Jesus at play. With a searching gaze He rebuked the lads and they fell dead on the spot.

Ever since those ancient paintings which portray Jesus crowned with a halo, Christians have tried to free Him from His own humanity. But the Gospels will not allow it. Jesus was unique, for He was the manifestation of God Himself. But He was also perfectly human. His acceptance of our finitude means that He submitted to His parents' admonition and correction. Jesus went through all the normal stages in the development of His body, mind, and spirit. The incarnate God's willing acceptance of the limitations of our humanity is part of the mystery of the divine condescension. The "Incarnation" as Luther once said, "defies our understanding."

C. S. Lewis, who had a gift for expressing Christian truth simply, once wrote:

The Second Person in God, the Son, became human Himself: was born into the world as an actual man—a real man of a particular height, with hair of a particular colour, speaking a particular language, weighing so many stone. The Eternal Being, who knows everything and who created the whole universe, became not only a man but (before that) a baby, and before that a fetus inside a woman's body. If you want to get the hang of it, think how you would like to become a slug or a crab (*Mere Christianity*, © 1943, 1945, 1952 by Macmillan Publishing Company, Inc., p. 140).

The Purpose of the Incarnation

Hopefully, the question "Who is Jesus?" is now clear. He is both God and man. But in the New Testament who Jesus *is,* is seldom divorced from what He *does.* The "person" and the "work" of Christ form an inseparable whole.

It comes as no surprise then to discover that the *Logos* invaded our planet for one supreme purpose: to save a lost human race from eternal ruin. For us and for our salvation Christ became in all respects a man. That is why Gregory of Nazianzus told the fourth-century Apollinarians, who denied that Christ had a human soul, that whatever Christ did not assume, Christ did not heal.

Hebrews 2:9-18 unfolds six reasons why Jesus Christ was "made for a little while lower than the angels":

(1) That He might taste death—the wages of sin—for every man (v. 9). Our Lord's suffering was substitutionary. He died in our stead that we might live.

(2) That He might bring many sons to glory (v. 10). Christ descended to earth to lead the redeemed to the heavenly home. As Athenasius, the fourth-century bishop, put it, "He became what we are that He might make us what He is."

(3) That He might sanctify or set us apart as His brethren (v.

11). Christ's coming opened the door to a new relationship between God and man. Enemies can become His friends; aliens, privileged members of His family.

(4) To destroy the power of the devil (v. 14). Christ came to earth and suffered to loose men from the bondage of sin. Satan's control over the human heart was broken by Christ's life, death, and resurrection.

(5) To deliver us from the torment of death (v. 15). Death died at the death of Christ. Hence, the believer no longer fears the sting of the grave.

(6) To become a perfect high priest for the propitiation of sins (v. 17). The sin which alienated man from God was cleansed forever by the self-sacrifice of the incarnate Lord.

Anselm, Archbishop of Canterbury, concluded in *Why God Became Man,* that the second Person of the Godhead entered the world not out of curiosity, nor out of any sense of personal need. The Father sent the Son on an errand of mercy solely to accomplish man's redemption. Since man was created by the Word (John 1:3), it was fitting that fallen man should be recreated by the same Word (John 3:17). Perhaps Paul expressed the primary purpose of the Incarnation best when he said, "Christ Jesus came into the world to save sinners" (1 Tim. 1:15).

Values of the Incarnation

The fundamental reason for the Incarnation was man's salvation, yet the coming of Jesus Christ in flesh also highlights several other important spiritual truths. The first is that the Incarnation demonstrates the dignity of human life. Not everyone in the ancient world believed that. Plato and other Greek philosophers held that human flesh is despicable, and the early Docetists believed that God, the pure Spirit, could have nothing to do with our material bodies. The coming of Jesus, however, points up man's significance.

During his imprisonment by the Nazis, Dietrich Bonhoeffer witnessed a great deal of man's inhumanity to man. So brutal was the punishment in those concentration camps that many prisoners despaired of man. Was man any more than a beast? Yes, said Bonhoeffer, in *Letters and Papers From Prison.* The German martyr argued that if God did not despise sinful humanity, how can we? "God Himself did not despise humanity, but became man for man's sake."

The holy God did not despise our human form. No, He ordained that His own Son should assume our mortal flesh. All the weaknesses, impulses, and temptations common to our manhood He took to Himself and sanctified. The Incarnation, therefore, demonstrates the worth of sinful man. It separates man from the soulless beasts.

A second lesson the Incarnation teaches is that sin is not a normal quality of human life. Jesus Christ became man and lived a perfect, sinless life. In thought, word, and deed He was a man marked by selflessness, compassion, and purity. The Christian, therefore, finds it necessary to reject the common saying, "to err is human." A look at Jesus persuades us that sin is flatly subhuman. The unregenerate person is less than fully human, but the believer in Christ recovers his authentic humanity as he is transformed by the Spirit into the likeness of Christ (2 Cor. 3:18).

The incarnate Lord, then, furnishes a model for a Christian's life in the world. The altogether holy God, through the person of His Son, identified with this sinful world. Through Jesus, God entered the world, our real world, that He might minister to its needs. The Lord Jesus mingled with harlots, publicans, and sinners to bring them the bread of life.

Outwardly, Jesus identified completely with a God-rejecting world; inwardly, He remained unstained from every appearance of evil. Now, God summons the Christian to walk in the steps of His Saviour. The Lord doesn't ask the believer to insulate Himself from the world. But after the pattern of Jesus, he is to relate to a bruised and hurting world that the Gospel might shine into every corner of society. The disciple's goal is to be "in the world, but not of the world."

One final merit of the Incarnation remains. The veiling of the Word in flesh upholds an ethical model. The prophet Isaiah foresaw in the humiliation of the Christ the embodiment of true servanthood (Isa. 52:13ff.). For the Apostle Paul the Incarnation represented the highest expression of self-renunciation (Phil.

2:3ff.) and condescending grace (2 Cor. 8:9). Peter saw in Christ's coming the supreme example of obedience to the will of God for the sake of others (1 Peter 2:21-24). And John could say, "In this is love, not that we loved God, but that He loved us and sent His Son to be the propitiation for our sins" (1 John 4:10). As we meditate upon the love and grace of the Christ who became man, the Word of God addresses each one of us: "Let Christ Jesus be your example as to what your attitude should be" (Phil. 2:5, PH).

5

Offspring of Mary

It was a crucial moment in human history. The eternal God stooped to favor an obscure Jewish maiden who was perhaps 15 years of age. God might have chosen a well-bred, richly clad woman from among the Jerusalem elite. Instead He chose a humble country maiden to be the mother of His own Son, our Saviour.

"Conceived by the Holy Spirit"

The angel Gabriel told Mary that she would conceive and bear a Son named Jesus. But the girl from Galilee was troubled. She was engaged, not married. The angel reassured Mary with the promise, "The Holy Spirit will come upon you, and the power of the Most High will overshadow you; therefore the child to be born will be called holy, the Son of God" (Luke 1:35, RSV).

When Mary returned to Nazareth after a visit with her cousin Elizabeth, Joseph was shocked to learn that his fiancee was expecting a child. The Law allowed Joseph to expose Mary and have her stoned, but he was hesitant to take this action. While weighing the matter, an angel spoke to him in a dream. "Joseph, son of David, do not be afraid to take Mary as your wife, for that which has been conceived in her is of the Holy Spirit" (Matt. 1:20). Joseph obeyed God without hesitation. He legalized their marriage but didn't "know" his wife until she had delivered the baby.

"The Christmas miracle," as one theologian called it, is familiar to us all. In a dingy cow stall in Bethlehem the virgin Mary brought forth her firstborn. No sterile delivery room for the Lord's Anointed! To the outward eye here was a baby of flesh and blood who was nourished by his mother's own life. But to the eye of faith the child was different. He was God's own Son. While worldlings wined and dined in the comfortable inn, the God-fearing couple worshiped the Lord who had favored them so graciously.

By its very nature the Virgin Birth was hidden to public view. Joseph and Mary were reluctant to speak of this miracle openly, particularly in the presence of their other children. Some time passed before the Virgin Birth became the common knowledge of the church. Nevertheless, believers confessed its validity in the Apostles' Creed, which spoke of "Jesus Christ His only Son our Lord, who was conceived by the Holy Spirit, born of the Virgin Mary. . . ."

The term "virginal conception" is perhaps more precise than "virgin birth." The absolutely unique feature of this event was Mary's conception by the power of the Holy Spirit apart from male agency. The term "virgin *birth*" was coined in the Early Church to counter the Gnostic claim that Jesus was "poured through" the womb of Mary. Jesus' birth by Mary is proof that our Lord was no phantom. His was a genuine physical body.

Jesus' virgin birth is at once a miracle and a mystery. Medically, conception without male agency is incredible. It has no documented parallel in the annals of medical science. Yet the Christian is not baffled by the event. The God of the Bible is the God of miracles. As Luther once said in a Christmas sermon, "The Virgin Birth is a mere trifle for God; that God should become man is a greater miracle."

Science, in spite of all its achievements, has yet to originate life. How much more mysterious, then, is the virginal conception of the Son of God. Scripture acknowledges the essential mystery of our Lord's earthly origin (1 Tim. 3:16). Yet as one observer has noted, "The presence of mystery is the footprint of the divine."

Have we ever considered what would have happened if Mary and Joseph had lived in our day, in our kind of society? The plain fact is that Jesus might never have been born! Consider Mary pregnant by an unknown father. The modern social worker or counselor would likely recommend a quick abortion. Or consider her claim of having conceived through the power of the Holy Ghost. Surely Mary would be a prime candidate for psychiatric treatment. Malcolm Muggeridge, the English social prophet, astutely concludes: "Our generation, needing a Saviour more, perhaps, than any that has ever existed, would be too humane to allow one to be born; too enlightened to permit the Light of the World to shine in a darkness which grows ever more oppressive."

I Can't Believe That!

In the early church the Virgin Birth was upheld as a universal truth. Only a heretic such as Cerinthus, who lived in Asia Minor at the end of the first century, could teach that Jesus was an ordinary son of Joseph and Mary. He was a forerunner of later Gnostic teachers who rejected Jesus' virgin birth on the belief that a holy God could not possibly contact sinful flesh. The point is that the early church was united in its rejection of such reasoning. Only heretics outside the fold of faith dared to voice their denial.

The Madonna, that painted or sculptured figure of the virgin Mary glowing with spiritual beauty as she embraces the Christ Child, is more representative of early Christianity, for the presence of thousands of Madonnas in the churches and cathedrals of Europe witnesses to Christendom's near universal belief in the Virgin Birth.

Time, however, brings changes. Today attacks against the Virgin Birth often originate from within the Church. Many liberal theologians and clergy have difficulty believing the doctrine. Harry Emerson Fosdick, the well-known liberal preacher, once said to his congregation: "I want to assure you that I do not believe in the virgin birth of Christ, and I hope none of you do." Such a conviction springs from the view of Jesus as a mere man. One has no need of the Virgin Birth hypothesis to account for an ordinary mortal.

Emil Brunner, a modern Swiss theologian, believed in Jesus' Incarnation but not His Virgin Birth. He argued that the idea was invented by some early Christians who wanted to explain the Incarnation in biological terms for believers weak in faith. Brunner concluded that "the doctrine of the Virgin Birth, like the doctrine of the inspiration of the Bible, is a danger to the Christian faith."

Other critics of this doctrine dismiss the Virgin Birth as a myth or legend. The ancient pagan world recounted fantastic tales of gods such as Zeus who cohabited with women to produce creatures half human and half divine. The achievements of ancient heroes like Cyrus, Augustus Caesar, and Alexander the Great were commonly attributed to some sort of supernatural birth. According to one legend, Caesar's mother was asleep in the temple of Apollo when she conceived through the agency of a serpentlike god. But such bizarre fables have little in common with the biblical account of the virginal conception of Jesus of Nazareth.

Modern-day cults which deny Jesus' deity discount, of course, His conception by the Holy Spirit. Sun Myung Moon, for instance, believes that Mary became pregnant because she was unfaithful to Joseph. Moon is uncertain whether Mary was unfaithful to her fiance only once or many times. In any case, he claims, Jesus was an illegitimate child.

During a recent Christmas season two Danish pastors discussed the birth of Jesus on state television. The pastors felt that it was inconceivable that Mary conceived by the supernatural agency of the Holy Spirit. Before a large holiday audience the pastors concluded that Jesus was the illegitimate child of a Palestinian harlot. Such an idea, unthinkable to an apostolic Christian, is not new. One strand of ancient Jewish tradition taught that Jesus was born out of wedlock. Most Jews, though, believe that Joseph was Jesus' natural father.

How does one account for the widespread rejection of the Virgin Birth in our day? Overemphasis upon God's immanence is one factor. Scripture teaches that God exists beyond the temporal realm (transcendence) and that He also indwells the world and its processes (immanence). Modern thinking tends to neglect the transcendent reality of God. The Creator, so we are told, always works within the ordinary processes of nature. Because God is at work *in* the world, one need not postulate any intrusion from *outside* the world. In this way the doctrine of the Virgin Birth is eliminated.

A second reason is the modern dominance of evolutionary dogma. According to this view, Jesus was not supernaturally conceived in the womb of the virgin. Rather, He was a genuine product of the evolutionary process with thousands of years of prehistory in His genes. Jesus represents the genuinely new in nature's progress toward higher levels of life. Of course, when Jesus is received as a product of biological evolution, the Virgin Birth is superfluous. But it is highly doubtful whether Jesus' unique self-consciousness or His lofty code of ethics can be accounted for by any evolutionary process. The biblical view of the unique incarnation and virgin birth of Jesus offers a more reasonable and coherent solution.

Pervasive antisupernaturalist attitudes are a further reason why the Virgin Birth has little significance in the modern world. In today's scientific era phenomena such as the Virgin Birth just don't happen. Modern theologians have devised clever but fruitless arguments to explain away the Virgin Birth. Liberals argue that female rabbits have been shocked into conception without participation of males. Thus it is argued that Mary conceived through the shock of the angel's announcement. But through and through Christianity is a supernatural faith. Eliminate the breakthrough of the divine activity and Christianity reduces to religious humanism.

Old Testament Background

Following Jesus' resurrection the Gospels record several significant encounters between the risen Lord and His followers. On the road to Emmaus and later that night over dinner, Jesus taught the disciples that His birth, ministry, death, and resurrection were foretold in Old Testament Scripture. So Luke writes, "beginning with Moses and with all the prophets, He explained to them the things concerning Himself in all the Scriptures" (Luke 24:27). We should expect, then, to find intimations of Christ's unusual birth in the Old Testament. The initial announcement of the Gospel in Genesis 3:15 perhaps hints at the Virgin Birth. The future Messiah who would crush Satan is represented as Eve's "seed." Some interpreters such as Matthew Henry, regard Gen. 3:15 as a prophecy of the Virgin Birth. "He was to be the seed of a woman only, of a virgin, that He might not be tainted with the corruption of our nature." The language of the text does indeed suggest this.

Isaiah 7:14 is, of course, the classic Old Testament text: "The Lord Himself will give you a sign: Behold, a virgin will be with child and bear a son, and she will call His name Immanuel." To understand this verse we must consider its historical context. The kings of Israel and Syria in league together threatened to overrun Jerusalem. Yet God had not abandoned Judah. Indeed, God invited Ahaz to ask for a sign confirming the fact of divine protection.

King Ahaz, however, had already chosen the path of unbelief. He had determined to thwart the threatened assault from the north by enlisting the support of pagan Assyria. In turn, God responded that he would provide another sign, not for Ahaz, but for the entire house of David (Isa. 7:13). This sign was Immanuel Himself (Isa. 7:14).

Who was Immanuel but a child who was to be born, a son who would be given? (Isa. 9:6) He would be the shoot which would arise from the fallen house of David (Isa. 11:1). Ahaz looked to the Assyrian army to provide security. But God looked to the cradle of Bethlehem as the ultimate source of His people's peace.

Isaiah prophetically declared that Messiah would be born of an 'almah. Much debate surrounds the meaning of this Hebrew word. In short, 'almah signifies a young woman of marriageable age, assumed to be a virgin. When Matthew quotes Isaiah 7:14 he translates 'almah by the usual Greek word for virgin (Matt. 1:23). We may safely conclude that Isaiah predicted Messiah's birth of a virgin. An ordinary birth would hardly constitute a sign.

Martin Luther once said, "If a Jew or a Christian can prove to me that in any other passage of Scripture *'almah* means a married woman, I will give him a hundred florins, although God alone knows where I may find them."

New Testament Development

The most explicit teaching on the Virgin Birth is found in the Books of Matthew and Luke. So casually is Matthew's account of Jesus' birth introduced that it appears the facts were well known to his readers (Matt. 1:18-25). In the first Gospel the narrative focuses on Joseph, Mary's fiance. Matthew emphasizes that before their marriage was consummated Mary was found to be pregnant. While Joseph pondered the matter, an angel from God graciously told him that Mary had conceived through the power of the Holy Spirit, and that Joseph should take Mary as his wife and accept legal responsibility for their child. Mary's conception was no afterthought on God's part. Rather, it represented the fulfillment of God's eternal plan as witnessed by prophetic Scripture (Isa. 7:14).

In Luke's account (Luke 1:18-25), we are dealing with the narrative of a painstaking historian who carefully researched the facts of the case (Luke 1:1-4). Luke was also a physician eminently qualified to evaluate the circumstances of Jesus' birth. For these reasons the third Gospel is written from quite a different perspective than the first.

Mary occupies the center of the stage in Dr. Luke's account. She appears as a humble handmaiden who delights in the Lord her God. Graciously the angel Gabriel announces to Mary that she will be the mother of the Messiah, the glorious Ruler of Israel. Mary is thoroughly perplexed, for as yet she has no husband. The angel explains to her, however, how this extraordinary event will come about. "The Holy Spirit will come upon you, and the power of the Most High will overshadow you; therefore the child to be born will be called holy, the Son of God" (Luke 1:35, RSV). The expressions "will come upon you" and "will overshadow you" discount an ordinary conception. Luke affirms the mystery of Mary's virginal conception by the Holy Spirit without attempting to explain it.

The fact that both Matthew and Luke mention Joseph, Mary's husband, does not compromise the Virgin Birth. Joseph's inclusion highlights the importance of adoptive fatherhood in the Jewish mind. Both Gospels guard against identifying Joseph as Jesus' natural father. Matthew writes of "Joseph the husband of Mary, by whom was born Jesus" (Matt. 1:16). Luke includes the safeguard, "Jesus . . . being supposedly the son of Joseph" (Luke 3:23).

Critics allege that the rest of the New Testament is strangely silent on the Virgin Birth. Even if this were so, the argument from silence would prove nothing. We know that John, the disciple who leaned on our Lord's breast at the Last Supper, records nothing of this final event. In fact, however, the remainder of the New Testament is not entirely silent on the Virgin Birth. Its teaching on the subject is simply implicit rather than explicit.

Mark chose to begin his story of Jesus' ministry with our Lord's baptism. That is due to the fact that in the second Gospel Jesus is cast in the role of a servant—and who takes note of the birth of a lowly servant?

We might expect that John, "the beloved disciple," would have had some knowledge of the Lord's birth. John 8:12-59 seems to indicate that such was the case.

Jesus had just spoken to the Pharisees about his unique relation to the heavenly Father. The Jews in turn responded with a series of charges alleging Jesus' irregular birth.

First, the Pharisees challenged Jesus with the question, "Where is your Father?" (John 8:19) In other words, "Jesus, you don't know who your Father really is!" The Lord responded by claiming that *God* was His Father.

Second, the Pharisees snorted, "We were not born of fornication" (John 8:41)—the clear implication being that Jesus *was* born of fornication. Jesus responded with the claim that He came forth from God His heavenly Father.

Finally, the Jews charged Jesus with mixed Jewish-Gentile ancestry (John 8:48). Again Jesus could only testify that His paternity lay with God. No less than six times in this passage Jesus refers to God as "the Father" or "My Father" (vv. 19, 27-28, 38, 49, 54).

The same kind of allusions to the Virgin Birth mark the writings of Paul. Part of this is due to the fact that the New Testament Epistles were letters written to specific circumstances. With the possible exception of the Book of Romans, none was intended to be a systematic exposition of Christian doctrine. Nevertheless, in Paul's letters we do detect allusions to the supernatural character of Christ's birth.

In writing to the Romans, the Apostle referred to God's "Son, who was born of the seed of David according to the flesh" (Rom. 1:3). This is followed by the language of Romans 8:3, where God is seen "sending His own Son in the likeness of sinful flesh." Such an expression makes sense only in the light of the Virgin Birth.

The language used in Galatians 4 is especially suggestive. Twice in this passage Paul used the common word for an ordinary human birth: in relation to Ishmael (v. 23) and in relation to Isaac (v. 29). But when writing that "God sent forth His Son, born of a woman, born under the Law" (v. 4), Paul avoided the usual term denoting physical birth. Instead he used another word whose meaning is "to become" or "to come into being."

J. Gresham Machen, the great Princeton scholar of a former generation, concludes that "the Virgin Birth . . . is profoundly congruous with Paul's teaching about Christ." As we consider the total witness of Scripture we are compelled to agree with one theologian's judgment that "no one can dispute the existence of a biblical testimony to the Virgin Birth." One likely reason the Virgin Birth is not given more consideration in Scripture is that it was so universally accepted in the early church. No one calls attention to the obvious.

Practical Value of the Doctrine

How important is the Virgin Birth in the Christian scheme of things, after all? Can one be a Christian without believing the Virgin Birth? Briefly we want to consider the significance of the

Virgin Birth in relation to the Christian faith as a whole.

First, the doctrine is essential to a trustworthy Bible. If the biblical accounts of the Virgin Birth should be false, why should one hold to any other evangelical doctrine in Scripture? The Christian believes in the Virgin Birth because he holds God's Word to be true.

The Virgin Birth demonstrates that it is God who has taken the initiative in Christ. Jesus is God's great *gift* to mankind. The genius of the Gospel is that God *gave* His Son. Christianity depicts God stooping down to sinful men. Religion, on the other hand, is the story of man groping blindly after God.

Further, the Virgin Birth provides the only explanation of how the eternal *Logos* could become fully man without ceasing to be God. The offspring of a human union can only be human. Jesus' preexistence, Godhead, and resurrection from the dead necessitate a supernatural origin. Mary's conception by divine agency provides the only adequate basis for Jesus' sonship and Godhead (Luke 1:35).

The Virgin Birth is also related to our Lord's sinless human nature. The Holy Spirit mysteriously yet supernaturally sanctified Jesus' conception so that He was preserved from the contamination of fallen human nature. Luther put it this way: "Though Mary was conceived in sin, the Holy Spirit took her flesh and blood and purified them; and thence He created the body of the Son of God. . . . Thus He assumed a genuine body from His mother, Mary, but this body was cleansed from sin by the Holy Spirit. If this were not the case, we could not be saved."

This evangelical view corrects the Roman Catholic dogma of Mary's Immaculate Conception. Our Lord's mother shared our fallen nature. But her conception of Jesus was sanctified by the special activity of the Holy Spirit.

Finally, the reality of the Virgin Birth protects the integrity of Mary's character. Charges of unchastity leveled against the mother of our Lord are without foundation. Jesus was conceived by the Spirit apart from male agency.

It becomes clear, then, that we dare not adopt a "take it or leave it" attitude toward this Christian teaching. Theoretically, a sinner can accept Christ as Saviour without a clear understanding of the Virgin Birth. But we have seen that it is impossible to deny the Virgin Birth and at the same time hold to our Lord's preexistence, deity, sinless life, and resurrection. As J. Gresham Machen once said, "The Virgin Birth is an integral part of the New Testament witness about Christ, and that witness is strongest when it is taken as it stands."

6

The Unique
God-Man

There was once a skillful tailor who made a small fortune in his trade. When he was on his deathbed his friends in the business asked him the secret of his success. "Always," said the old man, "put a knot in your thread."

If we want to be effective in any endeavor we need to put the knot in our thread. It is even true of our faith. Christianity is delivered from meaningless religious motions because Jesus Christ is the knot in our thread. He is the unique revelation of God for all men for all time.

An Impossible Union?
Scripture teaches that in Jesus the heavenly and the earthly worlds unite. One might admit that Jesus was a man, or that Christ was God. But the confession that infinite deity united with finite humanity in a single person brings us to the very heart of the mystery of Christ.

Traditionally Christians have called the union of God and man in Jesus Christ "hypostatic union." The term is from Greek and means "personal." So complete, so indissoluble was this personal union that Christ is called not God and man, but the God-man. Our minds bog down before such teaching. How can deity with all its perfections be joined to humanity with all its limitations?

Daniel Webster, the 19th-century statesman, once dined in Boston with several eminent literary figures. Soon the conversation turned to Christianity. Webster, a convinced Christian, confessed his belief in Christ and His atoning work. A Unitarian minister at the table responded, "Mr. Webster, can you comprehend how Jesus Christ could be both God and Man?"

"No, sir, I cannot understand it," replied Webster, "and I would be ashamed to acknowledge Christ as my Saviour if I could comprehend it. He could be no greater than myself, and such is my conviction of accountability to God, my sense of sinfulness before Him, and my knowledge of my own incapacity to recover myself, that I feel I need a superhuman Saviour."

Many people, like the Unitarian minister, find it difficult, if not impossible, to believe that in Jesus of Nazareth God and man joined together. Frederich Nietzsche, the German philosopher, flatly declared that "a true man cannot at the same time be truly God." More recently, Paul Tillich claimed that the doctrine is a "Christology of absurdities." It is psychologically impossible, so the argument goes, for perfect God and imperfect man to constitute a single person. According to John A. T. Robinson the idea makes about as much sense as trying to place two billiard balls on one spot.

Quite a few moderns, then, deny the essential unity of Jesus and the Father. Christ, they tell us, differed from other men in *degree,* not in kind. He was more conscious of God dwelling in Him than we are. He was the special human vessel through whom God chose to work. But not God.

The question of how the authentic God could also be authentic man is by no means new. Back in the fourth and fifth centuries A.D. the church wrestled a great deal with the issue. Three leading controversies from these early days highlight the problem which faced the church.

Apollinarius (d. 390), bishop of Laodicea, held that at the Incarnation the divine Logos assumed a human body and soul, but not a human spirit. The eternal Word replaced the human spirit in Jesus. The Apollinarians, in effect, emphasized the deity of our Lord at the expense of His humanity. But a body and a soul without a spirit would be less than a complete man. Christ's sacrifice then, would have no redeeming effect on us.

Nestorius (d. 457) erred in the opposite direction. Although Christ's two natures were recognized, the integrity of their union was denied. Nestorians old and new hold to two natures in two persons, rather than two natures in one person. The idea is that of a play horse, where a cloth painted like a horse is draped over two people. In outward appearance the horse appears to be one, but in reality it is two. Nestorius himself said of Jesus Christ, "I hold the natures apart but unite the worship."

Nestorian Christians survive to this day in the South of India. Bishop Stephen Neill tells of a friend who once visited a Nestorian bishop in that part of the world. The conversation in due course turned to the doctrine of Christ. Said the Nestorian, "The union of the two natures in Christ is not like wine and water; it is like oil and water." Like oil and water! However vigorously you shake them, the oil always separates from the water. They remain two distinct entities, not one.

Eutyches, a monk from Constantinople (d. 454), propogated a third error. He held that like wine and water, Christ's deity and humanity mingled into one. Eutyches was once questioned about his doctrine by Flavian, archbishop of Constantinople. "Do you acknowledge Christ to be of two natures?" The monk responded, "I admit that our Lord was of two natures before the union, but after the union one nature, not two." In effect, Eutyches held that Christ's deity swallowed up His humanity so that the humanity was lost. Again Christ was reduced to less than a man. And the value of His sacrifice was compromised.

Henry Drummond, the influential Scottish preacher once said, "God does not make the mountains to be inhabited. We ascend the heights to catch a broader vision of our earthly surroundings. But we do not tarry there. The streams take their rise in these uplands, but quickly descend to gladden the fields and valleys below."

God, knowing the needs of men below, chose to descend to their level in order to save them. Man's struggle to explain this mystery only tends to magnify its uniqueness and makes it even more difficult to clarify.

The Union Confessed

In response to the early Christians' vain attempts to relate God-head and manhood in Christ, the church reexamined its belief in the light of Scripture. In the crucible of its life and mission, the church wrestled with the issues raised by the false teachers. Finally, 650 bishops of the church met at Chalcedon near Constantinople in A.D. 451 to discuss the union of the divine and human in Christ. The Council solemnly reaffirmed belief in the Nicene Creed (A.D. 325). Then they hammered out a statement of faith which spoke to the controversies of their own day. The resulting Chalcedonian Confession is the most significant statement on the Person of Christ ever produced. Because of its importance we quote from the heart of the statement:

> We confess and all teach with one accord one and the same Son, our Lord Jesus Christ, at once perfect in godhead and perfect in manhood, truly God and truly man . . . one and the same Christ, Son, Lord, only-begotten, proclaimed in two natures, without confusion, without change, without division, without separation; the differences of the natures being in no way destroyed on account of the union, but rather the peculiar property of each nature being preserved . . . not as though parted or divided in two persons, but one and the same Son and only-begotten God, the *Logos,* Lord, Jesus Christ.

What did the church confess about Christ back in the fifth century? Four things stand out: (1) His proper deity; (2) His authentic humanity; (3) the union of His divine and human natures in a single person—His person was fully integrated, not split or divided; and (4) the proper distinction of the two natures. In the union each nature retains its peculiar properties, as the creed put it, without "confusion," "change," "division," or "separation."

These four negative terms bring us to the crux of the problem. Together they guard against the various misrepresentations and heresies which have challenged the doctrine of Christ throughout history. Because they are so important we want to examine them.

First, deity and humanity united in Christ "without confusion." The properties of the divine and human natures did not mix in the union. The Incarnation produced no third substance. Second, God and man united "without change." The human in Christ was not swallowed up by the divine. Nor was the divine diminished by the human. As stated by one church father, Christ "combined both natures in a league so close that the lower was not consumed by the glory, nor the higher lessened by assuming lowliness." Third, the divine and the human in Christ exist "without division." Our Lord's two natures cannot be isolated or parceled out. Finally, the Person of Christ was constituted "without separation." Godhead and manhood have been forever joined together in Christ.

Two implications of the confession require a final comment. First, the Chalcedon Confession cautioned against dividing or separating the natures of the God-man. This implies that we should resist the temptation to attribute a given action of Jesus to one or the other nature. It might be tempting to conclude that as our Lord lay asleep in the stern of the boat or as He wept at Lazarus' tomb, His human nature prevailed. Or when He stilled the raging storm or walked across the lake His divine nature was dominant. The fact is that Scripture upholds *one* Lord Jesus Christ who was both God and man. Whatever Jesus did, He did as the God-man. Luther once said, "Often Christ is spoken of only according to the human nature, often only according to the divine nature, although what is said should be credited to both natures." Scripture nowhere encourages the separation of our Lord's person. Rather it consistently upholds the unity of His being (Mark 4:38-39; 9:7-8).

The second implication lies in the fact that the Chalcedon Confession defined the union of God and man in negative rather than positive terms. This observation underscores the essential mystery of our Lord's Person (Col. 2:2; 1 Tim. 3:16). By these negative terms the creed set up, as it were, four fences and declared that within this area lies the mystery of the God-man. Chalcedon didn't "solve" the classical problem of how deity could unite with humanity in a single person. At the human level the problem resists rational explanation. But the merit of the creed is that it establishes a boundary which distinguishes the biblical view from all others. Here lies the enduring value of the Confession. Living 1,500 years later, we may wish to say more in contemporary language. But we dare not say less than the church said then!

The Union Illustrated

Chalcedon confessed the union of the God-man without explaining the "how" of the process. Should we stop where Chalcedon stopped, or should we seek a formal explanation of how God united with man? Some in the church have tried to explain the process by the theory of Christ's "impersonal human nature."

The idea goes like this. God and man joined in the person of Jesus Christ. But each of these two natures could not have been personal, else there would be dual personality. The center of our Lord's life was the eternal *Logos*. Thus Jesus' humanity lacked a separate existence. The argument appeals to John 1:14, "the Word became *flesh*."

But is human nature without personality or ego a complete humanity? The early church raised this point in opposing the Apollinarians. On the other hand, if a human personality existed alongside the divine personality, the error of the Nestorians would lie at the door. It seems that our attempt to provide a logical explanation of the "how" of the hypostatic union breaks down. How the Son of God could simultaneously be the man of sorrows is beyond the reach of the human mind.

But certain analogies may help to illustrate the union. The church father Origen used the symbol of a glowing poker. As the heat permeates the iron, so Christ's humanity permeates the Word.

Luther preferred the analogy of the body and the soul. The body without the soul is incomplete, and vice versa. Yet the body and soul of a man are one. Luther was forced to admit that the union could not be explained. "Reason cannot comprehend this. But we believe it; and this is also the testimony of Scripture: that Christ is true God and that He also became a man."

The Christian should not be troubled by the presence of mystery in his faith. Wherever God and man meet, there is mystery. We should accept the doctrine of the unique God-man in the same way that we accept the Trinity—by faith in God's Word, the Bible.

Yet without Sin

As a real man Jesus shared our lot. Like us He was tempted to seek His own ends, to manipulate His neighbor, to deny His God.

Jesus felt the tug of temptation at the beginning of His public ministry. Following His baptism by John, Jesus was led by the Spirit into the wilderness where He fasted for 40 days. How hungry and weak He must have been after that ordeal! Yet then, when Jesus was most vulnerable, Satan attacked Him. All the trials and temptations of our Lord's three-year public ministry were heaped into one massive assault. How would the Son of God use His divine powers? To further His own ends? To defraud other people? To forge His own empire? The devil tried to destroy Him.

Satan first challenged Jesus to change stones into bread (Matt. 4:1-4). He was tempted to alter the course of nature to satisfy His physical needs. Here the Lord was tempted in body. Later Jesus was taken to a high turret of the temple and urged by the devil to cast Himself to the ground far below. Had not God promised that His angels would safely bear Him up? (Matt. 4:5-6) Here Jesus was tempted in mind. Finally, the Lord was led up a high mountain. From that vantage point Satan offered Jesus the world's kingdoms if only He would worship him instead of God (Matt. 4:8-9). In this trial Jesus was tempted in His innermost soul. Our Lord was tempted, then, in every respect as we are (Heb. 4:15), yet far more severely.

Jesus responded to Satan's subtle attacks by quoting Scripture (Deut. 8:3; 6:13, 16). Surrounded by Satan's snares, Jesus chose the path of perfect obedience to God. His life was the model of absolute sinlessness. John, the disciple who knew Jesus so intimately, bore witness to this fact (John 8:46; 1 John 2:1; 3:3). Paul spoke of Jesus as one "who knew no sin" (2 Cor. 5:21). Judas, full of remorse, testified that he had betrayed innocent blood (Matt. 27:4). The writer to the Hebrews clearly affirmed Christ's sinless character (Heb. 4:15; 7:26). And Peter described Jesus as "a lamb unblemished and spotless" (1 Peter 1:19). Napoleon, referring to the greatest figures in history said, "In every other existence but that of Christ, how many imperfections." Even the infidel Rousseau had to testify, "What purity in the manner of Christ."

Granted that Jesus *did* not sin, is it possible that Jesus *could* have sinned? The Bible does not answer this question directly.

But as we reflect upon the person of Jesus Christ we are inclined to reply, "No." An old maxim says, "To err is human." But our Lord's humanity must not be measured by ours. His was not a fallen nature, but a perfect one sanctified by the Spirit. Remember that Jesus was the unique God-man, the "same yesterday and today . . . and forever" (Heb. 13:8). At the center of His existence was the eternally pure *Logos*. In some mysterious way the divine nature of the God-man shielded His human nature against the possibility of sin.

A layman once asked his pastor about this problem. The preacher responded by raising the related question: "Could I beat my wife?" He then playfully flexed his arm muscle and said, "I think I could!" But he quickly added, "But, of course, you know I would never do such a thing."

Eyewitnesses of His Majesty

Shortly after Peter's confession of Christ near Caesarea Philippi, Jesus took Peter, James, and John up a shoulder of Mount Hermon to pray (Luke 9:28-36). We read that as the Lord was deep in prayer He was transfigured, or gloriously changed in appearance. Matthew records that "His face shone like the sun" (Matt. 17:2). In Luke's words, "the appearance of His countenance was altered" (Luke 9:29, RSV). The glory of God, like the brilliance of a heavenly body, shone through the face of the transfigured Lord.

We are reminded of Moses' appearance as he descended Mount Sinai after receiving the tables of the Law. "The skin of his face shone because he had been talking with God" (Ex. 34:29, RSV). Moses' experience differed from our Lord's in one significant respect. Like a mirror, Moses' face reflected the glory of God. But the brilliance on Jesus' countenance came from within. It was not a reflection.

The Gospels describe more of this extraordinary event. Luke recalls that "His clothing became white and gleaming" (Luke 9:29). Mark even more dramatically says, "His clothes became dazzling white, whiter than anyone in the world could bleach them" (Mark 9:3, NIV). Jesus' clothing, like His face, radiated like the glistening snows of Hermon. William Barclay notes that in Matthew's short account of eight verses, he uses the word "behold" three times, as if consumed by the sheer wonder of the sight (Matt. 17:1-8). Says Barclay, "From start to finish the keynote of this whole incident is glory."

Some suggest that at the Transfiguration Jesus' body was changed into a glorified body to highlight the majesty of the heavenly world. No, Jesus' humanity was not transformed into deity. What happened was that the divine glory which always shone in the depths of His being that one time radiated through the ordinariness of His person. The form of God glowed through the form of the servant. Did John have in mind this incident when he wrote, "We beheld His glory, glory as of the only begotten from the Father"? (John 1:14) Did the author of Hebrews think of the Transfiguration in his statement, "He is the radiance of His glory and the exact representation of His nature"? (Heb. 1:3) Peter surely recalled this moment on the mount when he wrote, "We made known to you the power and coming of our Lord Jesus Christ. . . . We were eyewitnesses of His majesty" (2 Peter 1:16).

We should probably regard the Transfiguration as a prelude to Jesus' passion. Before the crisis of the Cross, God certified that in His Son humanity and deity are one, suffering and glory are one, this world and the next are one. The brilliant outshining of heavenly glory proved that the One in whom God was well pleased (Matt. 17:5) was no ordinary man.

Peter's reaction to this glorious spectacle is interesting. The impetuous disciple said to Jesus, "It is good for us to be here; if You wish, I will make three tabernacles here, one for You, and one for Moses, and one for Elijah" (Matt. 17:4). Bishop McConnell says of Peter's hasty remark, "Peter belongs to the rather numerous class of persons who, when they don't know what to say, say it." One interpreter ventures that Peter's proposal suggests he wanted to create a monastic order with Jesus as leader. In any case, Peter wanted to prolong the experience on the mount. But God had a work for His Son to accomplish. He must descend the mount of glory and tread the path of suffering. The disciple too, like his Master, must leave the place of refreshment to face the demands of everyday discipleship. One of Susanna Wesley's favorite prayers captures this thought. "Help me, Lord, to remember that religion is not to be confined to the church or closet, but that everywhere I am in Thy presence." How perfectly was this ideal realized in the life of the unique God-man.

Practical Implications

Christians often overlook the fact that Jesus is now in heaven as the glorified God-man. Scripture teaches that Christ took His human form to the throne of God. "For there is . . . one mediator . . . between God and men, the *man* Christ Jesus" (1 Tim. 2:5). Paul knew that to represent men Christ must be the God-man. He must share the nature of both parties.

But 1 Timothy 2:5 emphasizes the God-man's humanity in relation to His ministry of mediation. He who pleads our case before the heavenly Father is our brother! He shared all our trials, afflictions and sorrows. Because of who He is, all the experiences of man become the experiences of God.

Scripture teaches that the God-man sympathizes with us in our trials and sufferings (Heb. 4:15). The word *sympathize* literally means to "suffer along with." Yes, the God-man in heaven suffers with us in our afflictions. When we hurt, He hurts too. How imperfectly we humans sympathize with those needy people around us. But because of the perfection of His deity and the reality of His humanity, our mediator is able to help and sustain those who are His (Heb. 2:18). He is the all-sufficient burden-bearer. Clarence Macartney, the Presbyterian pastor, once said, "If God was in Christ, and if He loved me and gave Himself for me, then all problems are solved and all wants are satisfied."

Our Lord's victory over Satan's temptations offers the possibility that the believer may daily triumph over the wiles of the devil. Nearly 2,000 years ago Jesus stood alone on earth before Satan and his cunning devices. But because the God-man now stands for us in heaven, the believer need not be terrified by his adversaries (Phil. 1:28, KJV). Because of the supernatural life of the God-man within, the Christian may emerge victorious from the deepest struggles with sin and Satan.

Probably all of us would have to admit that we have something of the fear and failure of Peter in us. Yet after Peter had fallen and been restored he wrote those words of great encouragement for us: "The Lord knows how to rescue the godly from temptation" (2 Peter 2:9). Armed with the Spirit of God and the Word of God, we follow in the train of the God-man and triumph through Him.

We have seen that when Jesus was transfigured on the mountain, the brilliance of God's glory permeated His entire being. Remarkably, the Apostle Paul took the word for Christ's transfiguration and applied it to the believer here and now. So he wrote to the Corinthians "And we all, with unveiled face, beholding as in a mirror the glory of the Lord, are being transformed into the same image from glory to glory" (2 Cor. 3:18). It is a law of life that we tend to become like those we behold. Paul made the staggering claim that as the believer contemplates the glory of God, he experiences a spiritual transformation similar to that of his Lord on the Mount of Transfiguration. Through the power of the indwelling Spirit, the Christian advances from one degree of glory to another. And this revolutionary transformation one day will be completed when we attain the likeness of the glorified God-man (1 John 3:2).

But supposing God became a man—
suppose our human nature which can suffer and die
was amalgamated with God's nature in one person—
then that person could help us.
He could surrender His will, and suffer and die,
    because He was man;
and He could do it perfectly because He was God.
You and I can go through this process only if God does
    it in us;
but God can do it only if He becomes man.

C. S. Lewis

7

Master Teacher

Jesus was the supreme Teacher. He often healed the sick, worked miracles, and sometimes preached. But His constant task was teaching. At least 45 times in the Gospels Jesus is called "teacher," but not once "preacher." Frequently we find statements such as, "He was going around the villages teaching" (Mark 6:6). Or, "He began teaching in their synagogues" (Luke 4:15).

When Nicodemus met Jesus, he said, "Rabbi, we know that You have come from God as a teacher" (John 3:2). The Lord Himself said to His disciples, "You call me Teacher, and Lord; and you are right, for so I am" (John 13:13). And Jesus' last word on earth was the command that His disciples should teach others as He had taught them (Matt. 28:20).

Jesus spent much of His time teaching individuals: Nicodemus, a woman from Samaria, the son of a Roman nobleman, a paralytic. But the Lord didn't restrict Himself to individuals. He seized the opportunity to teach a large crowd gathered on a hillside near Capernaum. During the Feast of Tabernacles He stood up and taught a throng of worshipers in the temple. And near the end of His life Jesus set aside several weeks for the instruction of His twelve disciples.

Wherever the opportunity presented itself, Jesus taught in a boat on the lake, in a remote Galilean village, or in a synagogue.

People recognized a difference between Jesus' teaching and that of the Jewish scribes who constantly appealed to the sayings of the rabbis. Matthew relates that "the multitudes were amazed at His teaching, for He was teaching them as one having authority" (Matt. 7:28-29). Luke recalls that the people were wondering "at the gracious words which were falling from His lips" (Luke 4:22). And John reports that certain officers readily confessed, "Never did a man speak the way this man speaks" (John 7:46).

Throughout the generations men have acknowledged Jesus' teachings as the most penetrating the world has known. Translated into more than 1,000 languages, they have transformed human lives and shaped the course of history.

The Character of Jesus' Teaching

The reader of the Gospels quickly discovers that Jesus' teaching was remarkably simple. He taught in such a way that children and ordinary folk understood Him. The universal appeal of His teaching is due to the fact that He expressed the most profound truths in elementary ways.

This simplicity of Jesus' teaching was due in part to its strikingly concrete form. Common, everyday objects were pressed into service to illustrate eternal truths. A fallen bird, a beautiful lily, a bushel basket, a lampstand, a grapevine, a coin—all made the truths about heaven more understandable to earthly ears.

Our Lord's message was also saturated with Scripture. So familiar was Jesus with the Old Testament that He was able to apply the Word of God in every situation. His first discourse in Nazareth, the Sermon on the Mount, and His cleansing of the temple were all hallowed with quotations from the Word. The Gospels record 33 direct quotations from 16 Old Testament books. From these references it appears that Jesus had a special preference for Deuteronomy, Psalms, and Isaiah.

The Scriptures were never lifeless platitudes to Jesus. He was too deeply involved with people for that. His teaching reflects profound insight into human nature. He knew man's attitudes, aspirations, and needs. As John notes, "He Himself knew what was in man" (John 2:25).

That is why His words were intensely personal, far more than a catalogue of facts. His message about the kingdom of God was always embodied in the life of the Teacher, because in the end Jesus came to give to men more than truths; He came to give Himself.

Jesus' Teaching Techniques

Most of Jesus' methods arose from life's situations. We might call one of these "the problem method." When Jesus forgave the sins of a paralytic some scribes posed the problem, "Who can forgive sins but God alone?" (Mark 2:7) In reply to the problem Jesus taught the onlookers about His divine authority to forgive sins.

Later, a rich young ruler approached Jesus with the question, "What shall I do to inherit eternal life?" (Mark 10:17) Jesus instinctively recognized a deeper problem, namely, the man's love of riches. So the Lord taught that to gain heaven one must be prepared to renounce all temporal possessions. The rich man turned to go, sadly, but Jesus seized the opportunity to teach the disciples about rewards (Mark 10:23-31).

Some time later in Jerusalem the disciples raised the problem of the time and circumstances of the temple's ruin (Mark 13:4). Jesus moved beyond the disciples' immediate concern and traced the complex events associated with His second coming in power and glory (Mark 13:5-36).

In addition to this "problem method" Jesus used personal conversations as a tool for teaching. He recognized the potential for shaping lives through informal discussions. Such a method calls for an ability to listen, as well as to talk, but Jesus knew how to use silence as well as shouts.

Once, a delegation of Pharisees and scribes engaged the Teacher in conversation in Galilee (Mark 7:1-13). The Jewish leaders were shocked that His disciples ate with ceremonially unwashed hands. Jesus denounced these supposed experts sharply: "You nicely set aside the commandment of God in order to keep your tradition." Citing the prophet Isaiah, He taught them that God requires true worship and obedience from the heart.

Perhaps the best-known use of the conversation method to

teach spiritual truth is in Jesus' encounter with Nicodemus. Talking with this Jewish ruler, Jesus taught that a man was fitted for heaven only by a spiritual rebirth. But when Nicodemus revealed an inability to grasp this truth Jesus told him directly: "God so loved the world, that He gave his only begotten Son" (John 3:16). Nearly always Jesus' conversations with people were brief, to the point, friendly, and personal. Sometimes they created friends, other times enemies. But always they communicated spiritual truth.

A third teaching technique was the use of leading questions. Francis Bacon once remarked that "the skillful question is the half of knowledge." Judging from the more than 100 questions recorded in the four Gospels, Jesus must have valued this method of teaching very highly. Our Lord's first recorded utterance was a question. When His parents found Him in the temple He asked, "Didn't you know I had to be in My Father's house?" (Luke 2:49, NIV) And one of His last was a questioning cry to the Father, "My God, My God, why have You forsaken Me?" (Mark 15:34, NIV)

Jesus also asked questions to incite interest. To the man paralyzed for 38 years Jesus put the probing question, "Do you wish to get well?" (John 5:6) To kindle the interest of the crowd gathered by the sea Jesus asked, "How shall we picture the kingdom of God?" (Mark 4:30) From that point He proceeded to teach the people in parables.

An appropriate question often prompted people to more serious thinking. Enroute to Jerusalem, the disciples reminded Jesus that they deserved top cabinet posts in His kingdom. The Lord responded with the thought-provoking question, "Are you able to drink the cup that I drink, or to be baptized with the baptism with which I am baptized?" (Mark 10:38)

Sometimes Jesus raised questions to confound His opponents. After a synagogue service He healed a man afflicted with dropsy. Anticipating the ire of the onlooking lawyers and Pharisees, Jesus raised the question, "Which one of you shall have a son or an ox fall into a well, and will not immediately pull him out on a Sabbath day?" (Luke 14:5) Since scribal law granted this exception, the Jewish officials were unable to reply.

Jesus also raised questions to challenge people to action. On one occasion He asked those who heard His teaching, "Why do you call Me 'Lord, Lord,' and do not do what I say?" (Luke 6:46) Later the resurrected Saviour appeared to Simon Peter and asked him three times, "Do you love Me?" (John 21:15ff.) This prepared the way for Jesus' call, "Tend My sheep" (John 21:17).

A fourth method of teaching, used especially with larger groups, was the lecture method. We find Jesus using it on the mountain, in the open country, by the seaside, or in the temple. He often taught His disciples this way. Before sending out the Twelve, He told them to whom they were to go, what they were to say, the provisions they were to take, and how they were to act when mistreated (Matt. 10:1-42).

One of the longest discourses recorded in Scripture is Jesus' tender farewell address in the Upper Room (John 14—16). In this moving message Jesus taught His followers about their heavenly home and the Comforter who would minister to them. He told them God's requirements for fruit-bearing and the persecution they would face in a hostile world. The disciples, who were struck by the clarity of Jesus' talk, responded, "Now you are speaking clearly and without figures of speech" (John 16:29, NIV).

Finally, we may note that in order to put truth in concrete form rather than abstract, Jesus taught by means of simple object lessons. For instance, he pointed to a fallen sparrow to illustrate God's providential care for His children (Matt. 10:29). He referred to an old wineskin to point up the impossibility of putting new life in an old vessel (Matt. 9:17). A widow's two copper coins symbolized selfless, sacrificial giving (Mark 12:42-44). A lost sheep exemplified the sinner's helpless condition (Luke 15:3-7). A grain of wheat fallen in the soil illustrated the principle that death to self must precede spiritual life (John 12:24). And fishermen working their dragnets symbolized the end-time separation of the just and the unjust (Matt. 13:47-50).

Teaching by Parables
Probably the most unique feature of Jesus' teaching, however, was the parable. A parable is a graphic story, true to nature and

human experience, which illustrates some spiritual truth. About 35 parables of our Lord are preserved in the Synoptic Gospels. With its vivid imagery and economy of words the parable functions like a mental puzzle challenging the listener to discover its hidden meaning.

Considering the other methods at His disposal, why did Jesus so often teach by parables? The disciples raised this question after the Lord told the parable of the sower. Jesus' response deserves attention. "To you it has been granted to know the mysteries of the kingdom of heaven, but to them it has not been granted. For whoever has, to him shall more be given, and he shall have an abundance; but whoever does not have, even what he has shall be taken away from him. Therefore I speak to them in parables; because while seeing they do not see, and while hearing they do not hear, nor do they understand" (Matt. 13:11-13).

Our Lord implied that the parables served a twofold purpose. To the receptive and spiritually minded, parables disclosed the Gospel. To the unreceptive and carnally minded, parables served to conceal the truth. These stories were sufficiently clear to instruct those who were willing to hear. Yet they were sufficiently opaque to puzzle those unwilling to obey the truth.

Jesus was a master strategist. Had He spoken plainly, His opponents would have turned on Him and ended His ministry all too soon. So Jesus veiled His teaching to the hard hearted through parables (Matt. 13:14-15). In His own terms, Jesus was reluctant to give what was holy to dogs or to cast pearls of truth before swine (Matt. 7:6).

The parables can be classified in various ways. One helpful way is a twofold division: Ethical parables and Kingdom parables. In both cases, however, proper interpretation demands that we resist the temptation to attach exotic spiritual meanings to all the details of the story.

The parables were designed to communicate one major spiritual truth. Among the ethical parables, the story of the good Samaritan (Luke 10:29-37) teaches that the heart of true religion is loving concern for one's neighbor. The parable of the rich fool (Luke 12:16-21) illustrates the ultimate folly of worldly success. The account of the prodigal son (Luke 15:11-32) is regarded by many as the world's greatest short story. It affirms the heavenly Father's forgiving grace toward wayward sinners. The parable of the unmerciful servant (Matt. 18:23-35) teaches that those who have received God's forgiving mercy should freely forgive others. The parable of the talents (Luke 19:11-27) teaches that the believer's heavenly reward is proportional to the degree of his commitment to Christ here on earth.

The "Kingdom parables" designation is due to the fact that 17 parables in the New Testament specifically mention the kingdom of God. They unfold the character of the Father's rule in its origin, development, and consummation.

The parable of the sower (Matt. 13:3-8, 18-23) indicates the kinds of reception people give the message of the kingdom. The four kinds of soils—the trodden path, rocky ground, thorny ground, and good soil—symbolize, respectively, the stubborn, the shallow, the selfish, and the saved. The parable of the wheat and tares (Matt. 13:24-30) teaches the coexistence of the righteous and the unrighteous until the final separation at the end-time judgment. The saying about the mustard seed (Matt. 13:31-32) illustrates the imperceptible growth of the kingdom from small beginnings. The parable of the leaven (Matt. 13:33) points up the kingdom's silent penetration of the present world order. The parable of the treasure hidden in the field (Matt. 13:44) highlights the priceless worth of the kingdom of God. To secure it one must be prepared to sell everything he has. The reality of a future judgment with eternal bliss for the believer and eternal torment for the unbeliever is the teaching of the parable of the dragnet (Matt. 13:47-50).

In each of the parables the hearer is expected to apply the story to his own life as an example or as a warning.

Jesus' Teaching on the Triune God

Whatever means He may have used, Jesus did not come to teach a new religion or encourage worship of some new god. He proclaimed only the God of Abraham, Isaac, and Jacob (Mark 12:26). Throughout His ministry His teaching about God reflected

His roots in the Old Testament. He felt at home reciting the traditional Jewish Shemah: "Hear, O Israel; The Lord our God is one Lord" (Mark 12:29).

The God Jesus worshiped is spirit (John 4:24), sovereign (Mark 12:27), holy (John 17:11), gracious (Matt. 7:11), and just (Luke 11:42). But according to the Nazarene, perhaps God's chief attribute is His love (John 5:42). The parables of Luke 15—the stories of the lost sheep (vv. 3-7), the lost coin (vv. 8-10), and the prodigal son (vv. 11-32)—tellingly illustrate the love of God.

In the Old Testament God is revealed primarily as the sovereign King. But Jesus taught about a God whose intimacy with His people is best expressed by the Father-son relationship. The Old Testament saint didn't think of God as his Father. But Jesus did.

In all of His prayers except one Jesus referred to God as His Father (Matt. 11:25; 26:39, 42). So intimate was this relationship that Jesus instinctively spoke of God as Abba ("daddy"), a word usually found on the lips of a trusting child (Mark 14:36). And Jesus taught believers that God was their heavenly Father too (Matt. 5:45; 6:26; 10:20).

Within the unity of the Godhead Jesus also recognized a plurality of divine persons. The "Holy Spirit" (Luke 11:13), also called the "Spirit of truth" (John 14:17; 15:26), is one in being and activity with the Father. Jesus taught that all His works of exorcising demons, healing the sick, and raising the dead were accomplished through the power of the Spirit. The Spirit, moreover, exercises a profound ministry in the world. He has come to "convict the world concerning sin, and righteousness, and judgment" (John 16:8).

Jesus taught us that, if a sinner freely allows the Spirit to dwell in his heart, he will find perfect satisfaction from spiritual hunger and thirst (John 4:14; 7:38). Yet continued stubborn resistance to the Spirit's working amounts to blasphemy and is beyond the reach of forgiveness (Matt. 12:31-32).

According to Jesus the ministry of the Spirit is the lifeblood of the church. He taught that after His departure, the Spirit would empower believers for effective service in the world (John 20:22-

23; Acts 1:8). In Old Testament times the Spirit of God inter-
mittently came and went. But after Jesus was glorified, the Spirit
came as a permanent Comforter. He now guides the believer into
all truth (John 14:26; 16:13), testifies to the reality of Christ
(John 15:26), and bestows all grace (John 16:15). In short, the
Holy Spirit takes the place of the earthly Jesus and inaugurates a
new era of spiritual power.

Dr. J. H. Jowett, the famous English preacher, once talked to
an old, experienced sailor about his ship. "Will you explain to me
the phenomenon of the wind?"

"I don't know what you mean, sir," the seaman replied.

"Well, how do you explain the wind which propels your great
ship?"

"I don't know anything about the wind," the sailor said, "but
I can hoist a sail!"

Just so the Christian may not be able to explain the working
of the Holy Spirit, but he can experience the Spirit's power in his
own life and ministry (John 3:8).

Jesus added to this teaching about the Holy Spirit certain basic
truth about His own person and mission. He told His disciples
that He possessed a unique relation to the heavenly Father. On
one hand, He made the awesome claim of total equality with God
the Father (John 14:10; 16:15). On the other hand, Jesus recognized His subordination to the Father: "The Father is greater than
I" (John 14:28). Thus, the New Testament suggests that Jesus was
equal to the Father in being and nature but subordinate in terms
of the work He performed.

Jesus also taught that He had a special mission to perform in
the world (John 16:28). He preached the Gospel of the kingdom
of God and urged repentance (Mark 1:14-15). His mission, He
said, was to seek the lost (Luke 19:10). But the ultimate purpose
and goal of Jesus' life was death on the cross (Matt. 16:21). Jesus
was born to die.

Jesus' Teaching on Scripture and the Law
Undergirding all that He taught was Jesus' high view of the Scriptures. In His great high priestly prayer Jesus petitioned the Father

for His disciples. "Sanctify them in the truth;" He prayed, "Thy word is truth" (John 17:17). Earlier, when challenged by the Jews, the Lord simply said, "Scripture cannot be broken" (John 10:35). It is clear that Jesus implicitly accepted the full authority of Old Testament "Scripture" (John 7:38; Matt. 22:29).

Significantly, Jesus apparently accepted the historicity of several disputed Old Testament events: Jonah's experience in the belly of a fish (Matt. 12:40-42), for example, along with Noah's ark and the flood (Luke 17:26-27). The only sensible conclusion one can draw is that Jesus upheld the entire truthfulness of the Old Testament.

Jesus' attitude to the Law, however, was unusual in His day. He said on one occasion: "Do not think that I came to abolish the Law or the Prophets; I did not come to abolish, but to fulfill. For truly I say to you, until heaven and earth pass away, not the smallest letter or stroke shall pass away from the Law, until all is accomplished" (Matt. 5:17-18). In effect Jesus claimed that not a single letter of God's Law would be annulled. The Law is so sacred that every precept would be fulfilled or perfectly filled out.

In significant ways Jesus' view of the Law also differed radically from that of the scribes and Pharisees. The religious experts of His time surrounded God's Law with thousands of minute rules and regulations. The result of their work is the Talmud, a Jewish commentary on the oral traditions built up around the Law. The Babylonian Talmud comprises no less than 60 printed volumes. Unlike the rabbis, Jesus was not concerned with such legalistic amplifications of the Law (Mark 7:8-9, 13). He fulfilled the Law perfectly, not by slavish obedience to the letter, but by working out the spiritual principles contained in it.

The Sermon on the Mount provides several vivid examples. In this message to His followers Jesus extended the commandment on murder to include anger (Matt. 5:21-22). Similarly, adultery, He said, is not merely an outward act but an inward thought (Matt. 5:27-28). The Law, they knew so well, prescribed "eye for eye, tooth for tooth" (Ex. 21:24). But Jesus condemned retaliation of any sort (Matt. 5:38-42). And, throughout the Sermon the frequent saying of our Lord, "But I say to you," highlights the authority that He, the Son of God, possessed in unfolding further dimensions of the divine will.

This one sermon on the mountain helped to create Jesus' reputation as the Master Teacher *par excellence*. He uttered the loftiest truths human ears have ever heard. But the Sermon also reveals that behind the spoken word was always the man Himself. Jesus' greatness as a Teacher was due to the fact that His teaching arose from the person who declared, "I am the truth" (John 14:6).

8

Model Servant

Paul Tillich, the late German theologian, spent his life teaching others about God. But in a recent biography entitled *From Time to Time,* Tillich's widow reveals the sordid and sensual character of the man's personal life. The radical theologian could never appeal to others to make his life their model. Not so Jesus. Without qualification the Lord could command His followers both to "do as I say" and to "do as I do." He was not only the Master Teacher; He was also the Model Servant.

William Lecky, the 19th-century Irish historian, acknowledged that Jesus lived what He preached. "Christianity has given to the world an ideal character," said Lecky, "who throughout all the changes of the centuries has been not only the highest pattern of virtue, but also the chief incentive to its practice."

As we discovered in chapter 1, of the four Gospel writers, Mark alone presents Jesus as the active servant healing the sick, raising the dead, casting out demons. One way Mark stresses the constant labor of Jesus is to use the Greek word usually translated "straightway" or "immediately." The term occurs no less than 41 times in the Gospel, creating the impression of fast-paced action.

Scholars agree that Mark relied heavily on Peter for much of his information. Early in the second century a bishop named Papius reported that Mark served as Peter's interpreter and wrote his Gospel from the perspective of Peter's preaching. Support for this idea comes from the outline of Mark's Gospel which unfolds along the lines of Peter's words to Cornelius in Acts 10:38, "How God anointed [Jesus of Nazareth] with the Holy Spirit and with power, and how He went about doing good, and healing all who were oppressed by the devil; for God was with Him."

The same service theme is captured in the key text of the Gospel: "The Son of man did not come to be served, but to serve, and to give His life a ransom for many" (Mark 10:45).

Alexander Maclaren, one of the better-known biblical expositors of yesteryear, says of Mark's portrait of Jesus: "The principle seems to run through the Gospel of touching lightly or omitting indications of our Lord's dignity, and dwelling by preference on His acts of lowliness and service." That is why we must rely heavily on Mark for our understanding of Jesus as Master-Servant.

Old Testament Servant of the Lord

To fully understand Jesus' role as God's special Servant we must briefly consider the Old Testament foundations of the theme. The prophet Isaiah spoke of the nation Israel, collectively, as God's chosen servant. Israel had been summoned from among the nations to the Lord's service (Isa. 41:8-9). But the nation failed miserably in its sacred vocation. In spite of God's boundless mercies Israel proved a blind, dumb, and unprofitable servant (Isa. 42:18-25).

With Israel's failure the vision of the Servant of the Lord narrowed to a single figure—the chosen Messiah (Isa. 42:1-9). This Spirit-endowed Servant (v. 1) would be lowly, meek, and kind (vv. 2-3). He would establish justice in the earth (v. 4) and serve as a beacon to the nations who did not know the Lord (vv. 6-7). He would be the guarantor of a New Covenant between God and His people (v. 6). But Isaiah 49:7 indicates that the Servant would be despised, rejected, and condemned by the nation which had forfeited its lofty servant-calling.

Many regard Isaiah 52:13—53:12 as the most important passage in the Old Testament. Significantly, this key portion is a song about the life and suffering of the Messiah, the Lord's Servant. It opens with the Servant subjected to the deepest insult and humiliation (Isa. 52:14). Yet His suffering love has a redeeming effect upon the nations (Isa. 52:15).

The Servant is called the "Man of sorrows" because He is bruised and beaten for the world's transgressions (Isa. 53:3-5). He is so humiliated that Isaiah considers Him judged by God (v. 4). By some strange twist, however, the Servant's suffering and grief happen according to the divine plan. His whip-lashed body, like a stricken lamb, represents an offering for sin (v. 10). Through the Servant's patient endurance of this suffering a host of men and women are made righteous (Isa. 53:10-11). His hour of anguish provides eternal salvation for many others.

This prophetic portrait of the Messiah was in sharp conflict with Jewish opinion. Judaism anticipated a powerful, triumphant monarch who would vanquish its foes by sheer force. Isaiah's prophecy of a humiliated and suffering Servant was so foreign to their vision of the Messiah, that Jews came to view the Servant as the Jewish people as a whole. Judaism stumbled over a Messiah who in lowliness of mind came to suffer and to serve. Hence the Jews found it difficult to admit that messianic prophecy found fulfillment in Jesus of Nazareth.

Yet these Old Testament Servant prophecies were specifically applied to Jesus by the Apostles and early missionaries. Matthew saw in Jesus' compassionate deeds of healing fulfillment of the Servant prophecy recorded in Isaiah 42:1-4 (Matt. 12:17-21). Peter preached the miraculous deeds, death, and the resurrection of Jesus, God's "holy Servant" (Acts 3:13, 26; 4:27, 30). Later Philip preached Jesus to the Ethiopian eunuch by reading from Isaiah 53, the Servant prophecy (Acts 8:26-35). And, finally, in his first letter Peter alluded to Isaiah 53 in upholding Christ's patient endurance of suffering as the ultimate model of true servanthood (1 Peter 2:21-24).

From Old Testament prophecy, then, something of the attractiveness and appeal of Jesus, the Model Servant, begins to emerge. A Hindu once noted that although Muslims have been in India for more than 1,000 years, the Hindu would never say to a Muslim,

"I wish that you were more like Mohammed." On the other hand, he continued, Christianity has been in India only a quarter of that time. Yet there is no educated Hindu who would not say to a Christian, "I wish that you were more like Christ."

Jesus' Awareness of His Servanthood

Our Lord's baptism by John represented a decisive moment in His messianic career. Jesus' immersion in the waters of the Jordan was in no way a baptism of repentance for sins. He was the pure and spotless Lamb of God. Rather, His baptism was first a deliberate act of identification with the race He came to save. In addition, it marked the public assumption of His messianic office. The baptism represents Jesus' anointing by the Spirit for His divine mission. It was His first step of obedience as the submissive Servant of the Lord.

The Gospels record that as Jesus came up out of the water a Voice sounded from heaven, "You are My Son, whom I love; with You I am well pleased" (Mark 1:11, NIV). God's word of approval to His Son's act of consecration is a combination of two Old Testament Scriptures. "You are My Son," taken from Psalm 2:7, identifies Jesus as a King. The descent of the dove symbolizes the coronation of the royal sovereign. The words, "with You I am well pleased" are quoted from the Servant prophecy of Isaiah 42:1. The saying as a whole, then, designates Jesus as God's anointed Servant.

As our Lord launched His messianic career He was clearly aware of His royal status. But Jesus was no ordinary monarch surrounded by splendor, wielding the sceptre of sovereign power. The King came as a lowly Servant. In His humiliation the monarch would launch a mission of service and suffering. His was a sovereignty of perfect obedience to God and of undying love to man.

During His early ministry in Galilee Jesus visited the Nazareth synagogue on the Sabbath (Luke 4:16-21). In the midst of the service the Lord stood up and read from Isaiah 61:1-2. The reading dealt with the preaching and healing ministry of the Lord's Servant. At the end of the reading Jesus added, "Today this Scripture has been fulfilled in your hearing." In effect, Jesus said that the Servant motif outlined by the prophet Isaiah was the program of His own life and ministry.

Reports of Jesus' healing miracles in Galilee quickly circulated as far south as Judea. Since His miraculous deeds surpassed even the mighty works of Israel's greatest prophets, John sent two disciples to inquire whether Jesus was the coming Messiah. The Lord instructed the messengers to report what had taken place. "The blind receive sight, the lame walk, the lepers are cleansed, and the deaf hear, the dead are raised up, the poor have the Gospel preached to them" (Luke 7:22). Thus we learn that Jesus pursued a quiet ministry of healing and preaching, both reflections of the compassionate character of His messianic work.

The Lord's mission, however, was always endangered by misunderstanding. At Caesarea Philippi, when Peter boldly confessed Jesus as the promised Messiah (Mark 8:29) the Servant Saviour refused to speak of Himself as the "Messiah." More than that He discouraged others from using the title (Mark 3:12). Why this reticence from our Lord? Because during His earthly humiliation Jesus knew that He must suffer as a lowly Servant before He could be crowned as a King.

The disciples couldn't understand that. On the way to Jerusalem two of them, James and John, requested that in the heavenly kingdom they might occupy the places of honor, one on Jesus' right hand and the other on His left. The disciples were concerned about what they stood to gain by following Jesus. The Lord responded with a saying that must have pierced the disciples' hearts. "Whoever would be first among you must be slave of all. For the Son of man also came not to be served but to serve, and to give His life as a ransom for many" (Mark 10:44-45, RSV).

The disciples thought of greatness in terms of worldly success. From their carnal perspective, he is greatest who is served. But Jesus reversed the whole order of things. His own life was living proof of the rule that He who would be great must serve. In God's kingdom the greatest are the least and the least are the greatest. He who aspires to a place of honor in Christ's kingdom must imitate the Lord's lowly pattern of service and suffering.

Christ's Servant Ministry

In His hours with them Jesus tried to show His disciples that true greatness was in humility, generosity, and compassion. This servant attitude appeared in His ministry to the sick. In Galilee a leper forced his way into the presence of the Master and begged to be healed (Mark 1:40-45). The poor man was languishing in a squalid hut when he heard that the Healer had come to town. Although a loathsome sight, he made his way slowly toward the Lord. There were the putrifying sores, the flesh dropping off his bones, the smell of a diseased body, the haunted look of a wild beast in his eyes. His feeble voice cried out, "Depart! Unclean!" (see Lam. 4:15), for a leper was forbidden to come into contact with other people.

When the leper fell to the ground and cried out for healing, what did the Lord do? The Law forbade anyone except a priest to touch him. But moved by compassion Jesus bent over the leper and placed His fingers on the rotting sores. The leper was awed; no one had touched him for years. Yet in response to the poor outcast's faith, the Servant instantly cleansed him.

Such healings of untouchables illustrate the Servant's identification with the lowest and most degraded persons in society. The rabbis had a saying, that "when the Messiah comes He will be found sitting among the lepers at the gate of the city." Jesus was that Messiah!

Jesus preached the Gospel first and foremost. But He also fed the multitudes, healed the sick, and comforted the sorrowing. Out of a Servant's heart He ministered to the total needs of the publican, the harlot, the poor, the paralytic, and the demon-possessed. No sincere and humble heart was ever disappointed with Jesus Christ.

These miracles of healing serve another purpose, however; they were also "signs" of the kingdom of God which our Lord inaugurated by His coming. Through His acts of power evil was often routed, disease and death nullified, and Satan dealt a crippling blow. All this Israel's prophets foretold. In the New Age, they said, miracles would play a vital role in the ministry of the Lord's Servant (Isa. 35:5-6; 61:1). That is why believers found in Jesus that mighty Servant before whom the winds and waves were stilled and the demons fled.

Critics try to explain away Jesus' miracles as inventions of the early church or as later legends. Miracles are an offense to the liberal mind because they point to God as the only adequate cause of events.

Miracles, however, are more than a curiosity of the Christian faith. The miraculous fabric constitutes the very warp and woof of the Gospel. What is the greatest miracle of all, if not God's invasion of time in Christ for the salvation of His people? Christianity without miracles is no Christianity at all.

The Servant of the Lord, however, not only had power to save; He longed to save. His compassion was reflected in the story of the good Samaritan (Luke 10:29-37). The picture is familiar to Christians everywhere. The key point of the story is the question Jesus raised. "Who became a neighbor to the wounded man? Who cared enough to help the poor man who had been robbed, stripped, and beaten?" Not the priest, for when he came upon the victim he passed by on the other side of the road muttering as he went, "Poor fellow! Someone ought to lend him a hand. But not me; I'm late already for the synagogue service." The Levite was no help either. He hastened along in the steps of the priest.

Only a despised Samaritan cared enough to act. He tenderly bound up the victim's wounds, set the man on his own beast, and brought him to the safety of an inn. There the Samaritan cared for the man and even paid for his stay at the hotel.

Alexander Maclaren once observed that a heartless believer, so busy in the service of God that (like the priest and Levite) he does not bother to serve his neighbor, is a monstrosity.

The parable may be regarded as a commentary on the divine command, "You shall love the Lord your God with all your heart, and with all your soul, and with all your strength, and with all your mind; and your neighbor as yourself" (Luke 10:27). And who ever did that completely? Jesus embodied all that the parable teaches. The servant attitudes of mercy, love, and faithfulness were perfectly exhibited in Him.

Jesus also exercised a Servant-ministry to the sinful and the outcasts. Zaccheus was the head of a Roman revenue office in Jericho. In his collection of taxes he had dealt unjustly with the people. Because he became rich at the expense of the poor, he was hated by his fellow countrymen. Zaccheus, then, was the despised man of Jericho, a scoundrel—until Jesus got hold of him.

Luke records the story (Luke 19:1-10). When Jesus was passing through town, Zaccheus, out of sheer curiosity, climbed a tree. Hoping that he might catch a glimpse of the wonder-working rabbi, he found Jesus surrounded by people. As the Lord passed by the tree, however, He saw Zaccheus perched among the branches and called out, "Zaccheus, hurry and come down; for today I must stay at your home" (v. 5).

The notorious tax collector was startled by Jesus' summons. Not least of all because this was perhaps the first time since childhood that Zaccheus had heard his name uttered in tones of kindness. There was also that note of urgency in Jesus' voice: "Today I must stay at your home."

This is the only occasion when Jesus volunteered to be a guest at anyone's house. Why was He so eager to go home with a despised tax collector? Because a sinful man needed His mercy and forgiveness. That is why the Lord disregarded the taunts of the self-righteous Pharisees and ministered to Zaccheus' spiritual needs. The Servant of the Lord went to Zaccheus' house for the same reason that He took flesh and dwelt among us—to seek the salvation of sinners. "The Son of man has come to seek and to save that which was lost" (Luke 19:10).

Finally, we dare not overlook Jesus' humble Servant-ministry to His own followers, the disciples. The Lord's condescending act of washing His disciples' feet (John 13:1-5, 12-16) is symbolic of the whole tenor of His ministry. The scene was the Last Supper, when Jesus longed to fellowship with His followers and teach them before His departure. Luke tells us that the disciples came to this sacred meal arguing about who among themselves would be the greatest (Luke 22:24). Each was quite concerned about his personal prestige. None of the disciples, then, were minded to wash the dusty feet of the others as they entered the Upper Room.

During the course of the meal, Jesus was fully aware that "the

Father had given all things into His hands" (John 13:3). His was the absolute and universal dominion. He knew that just as He had come from God, so He would shortly return to God. His heavenly glory and majesty would soon be restored.

But what was Jesus' response to His imminent exaltation? Did He swell with pride? Or display His divine power? No, moved by sheer love (John 13:1), Jesus rose from the table, wrapped a towel about His waist, filled a basin with water, and washed the dirty, sticky feet of His followers. It was the job of a slave to wash the feet of guests before a feast. The disciples were too proud to stoop that low. But Jesus, the Model Servant, demonstrated through that lowly act that true greatness is the greatness of service.

A mechanic once submitted the plan of a new invention to a design engineer for evaluation. After careful study the engineer asked, "Have you made a model of the design?"

"No," the mechanic answered.

"Then," said the engineer, "I can't make a judgment on the matter. Your concept is no more than a theory. You've got to embody your idea in a workable model of wood and metal. Only that will verify your theory."

Christ claimed to be the Son of God in human flesh. But a skeptical world demands a flesh-and-blood demonstration of that awesome claim to deity. Jesus verified that claim by offering a perfect model of compassion, mercy, and kindness to multitudes of needy people. No one before or since has come close to providing a more workable model.

Christ Our Model

After Jesus had washed the disciples' feet and returned to the table, He unfolded the significance of His actions. The disciples acknowledged Him as Teacher and Lord. As Lord (Kyrios), Jesus was no less than the sovereign Ruler of the universe. As Teacher, His task was to guide the disciples in the paths of truth and right conduct. After identifying Himself in this way, Jesus then said to the Twelve, "If I then . . . washed your feet, you also ought to wash one another's feet" (John 13:14).

The clear implication of Jesus' statement is that if He, the God of heaven, stooped so low to serve, His followers ought to do the same. There was no mistaking His words: "I gave you an example that you also should do as I did to you" (John 13:15).

To this day, Jesus stands before His church as the Model Servant. In His person and ministry He exemplifies the virtues of compassionate servanthood. Jesus' final word to the disciples speaks to Christians of every age. "If you know these things, you are blessed if you do them" (John 13:17).

On the Thursday of Holy Week it is traditional for the Pope and his bishops to reenact the Upper Room foot-washing scene. Often the ceremony is performed as a religious stage play. For Christians, however, Jesus' act of foot-washing should be more than a ritual staged once a year. It should be the believer's pattern of servanthood every day of the year. As Peter declared, "Christ . . . suffered for you, leaving you an example, for you to follow in His steps" (1 Peter 2:21).

The life of Dr. Albert Schweitzer exhibited many servant qualities. Schweitzer was a brilliant musician, theologian, physician, historian, and writer. He could have achieved fame and security in any of these fields in his native Germany. Instead the gifted liberal renounced every worldly ambition and buried himself in what was formerly French Equatorial Africa. There in that hot and humid land he built his world-famous hospital.

Schweitzer ministered to the disease-ridden bodies of African tribesmen. He served the people as draftsman, carpenter, mason, dentist, counsellor, and teacher of his philosophy, "reverence for life." So deep was Schweitzer's "reverence for life" that he fed crumbs to ants and forbade the killing of insects. When the physician died in 1965 the world mourned for a man who had so freely given of himself for others. Yet neither Albert Schweitzer nor any other man can equal the humility, self-denial, and self-sacrifice of Jesus Christ, God's only begotten Son. He is the Supreme Servant.

9

Prophet, Priest, and King

Napoleon once ordered a coat of mail. When the craftsman finished it, he delivered it to the Emperor. Before taking it, however, Napoleon commanded the man to put it on. Then, taking a pistol, the Emperor fired shot after shot at the craftsman in the armor. It stood the test, so Napoleon paid him well.

The Mediator's Threefold Ministry

Throughout its history Israel was fashioning certain tests for the Messiah who was to come. After the Fall man languished under the evils of ignorance, guilt, and rebellion against God. But to overcome these vices God in His wisdom raised up in Israel the institutions of prophecy, priesthood, and kingship.

Early in Old Testament history God's chosen leaders often combined the functions of prophet, priest, and king. The Old Testament patriarchs, Abraham, Isaac, and Jacob, informally exercised these three offices as they proclaimed God's word, as they led in sacrifice, worship, and prayer, and as they ruled over their extended family or clan. Later Moses also, as the spokesman for the Lord, performed these three functions in Israel.

In David's day, however, the three offices formally developed into separate institutions. The prophet was divinely commissioned to proclaim the word of the Lord; the priest to minister before the

altar; and the king to rule upon the throne. All three were conse-
crated to office by anointing with holy oil: the prophet (1 Kings
19:16; Isa. 61:1-2), the priest (Ex. 30:30; 40:15), and the king
(1 Sam. 10:1; Ps. 45:7).

As the years passed, however, the institutions of prophecy,
priesthood, and royalty in Israel failed to meet the standards set
by God. Thus, the later history of Israel was a sorrowful tale of
false prophets, irreligious priests, and corrupt kings. This apostasy
during the closing centuries of Old Testament history provides the
background for a messianic hope that arose, searching for the
ideals of the true prophet, priest, and king.

Early Christians were convinced that these three offices uniquely
converged in Jesus. He is the Mediator (1 Tim. 2:5) who bridged
the chasm between a holy God and a sinful race by instructing,
atoning, and ruling.

The old Westminster confession describes Christ's threefold
ministry this way: "Our Mediator was called Christ, because He
was anointed with the Holy Ghost above measure; and so set
apart and fully furnished with all authority and ability, to execute
the offices of prophet, priest, and king of His church, in the estate
both of His humiliation and exaltation."

Christ's Prophetic Office

In Judaism a prophet was one commissioned to proclaim a message from God. The essential elements of biblical prophecy are
revealed in God's command to Jeremiah. "Before me you will
stand; . . . you will become My spokesman" (Jer. 15:19). From
this Scripture we see that the task of the prophet was twofold.
Passively, the prophet received a revelation of the divine will.
Actively, he related and interpreted the will of God to the people.
Luther once said, "That person is called a prophet who has an
immediate knowledge of God and into whose mouth the Holy
Spirit puts the Word."

The prophet's message was a complex one. On one hand, he
frequently spoke a revelatory word from God for the present. The
prophet reminded the people of the divine statutes, urged obedience to God, and warned of impending judgment. But the prophet

also spoke a predictive word for the future. He outlined the unfolding of events which the sovereign God would one day bring to pass.

The New Testament writers believed that Christ was the fulfillment and consummation of the line of Old Testament prophets. The prophetic ministries of Moses, Samuel, Elijah, Isaiah, Malachi, and John the Baptist all pointed to Christ. Christians came to see the prophetic institution in Israel as messianic in character. Calvin said that "the common office of the prophets was to hold the church in suspense, and at the same time support it until the advent of the Mediator."

The earliest intimation of Christ's prophetic ministry is found in Deuteronomy 18:15-19. "I will raise up a prophet from among their countrymen like you, and I will put My words in His mouth, and He shall speak to them all that I command Him" (v. 18). Although this text refers immediately to the line of Old Testament prophets, Peter declared that Moses ultimately spoke of Christ, the coming Prophet (Acts 3:22).

The prophet Isaiah also anticipated the Messiah's prophetic ministry with the prediction, "The Spirit of the Lord God is upon Me, because the Lord has anointed Me—to bring good tidings to the afflicted; He has sent Me . . . to proclaim liberty to the captives" (Isa. 61:1).

New Testament writers were certain that Jesus was the fulfillment of this Old Testament prophetic hope. In the Gospels the common people believed Jesus was a prophet. When the Samaritan woman realized that Jesus knew everything about her she confessed, "Sir, I perceive that You are a prophet" (John 4:19). Later, after the Lord had fed the 5,000, the astonished crowd remarked, "This is of a truth the Prophet who is to come into the world" (John 6:14; see also 7:40). And when Jesus entered Jerusalem on Palm Sunday the crowd was wild with frenzy. When asked who the rider on the donkey was, the people replied, "This is the prophet Jesus, from Nazareth in Galilee" (Matt. 21:11).

Our Lord Himself was fully conscious of His prophetic calling. When Jesus returned to a cool reception in Nazareth, He declared, "A prophet is not without honor except in his hometown"

(Matt. 13:57). On another occasion some Pharisees warned the Lord to flee Jerusalem or be killed by Herod. Jesus confidently responded, "It cannot be that a prophet should perish outside of Jerusalem" (Luke 13:33).

Christ's prophetic vocation is clearly reflected in the message He proclaimed. In His preaching and teaching Jesus claimed to have revealed the Father's Word to the world. On one occasion He entered the synagogue at Nazareth on the Sabbath, and by reading from Isaiah 61 He indicated that He was anointed to proclaim the Word of the Lord to the poor and the outcasts (Luke 4:18).

John's Gospel is filled with claims from the lips of our Lord that His teaching originated with the Father who sent Him into the world. He publicly declared, "I did not speak on My own initiative; the Father who sent Me has Himself given Me commandment, what to say and what to speak" (John 12:49). And later in the Upper Room the Lord reminded His disciples that "the word which you hear is not Mine but the Father's who sent Me" (John 14:24). Thus, in the tradition of Noah, that "preacher of righteousness" (2 Peter 2:5), and other godly Old Testament spokesmen, Jesus faithfully proclaimed God's revelatory word for the present. As the Apostle John put it, "the testimony of Jesus is the spirit of prophecy" (Rev. 19:10).

But as a prophet sent from God Jesus also spoke a predictive word for the future. Our Lord announced in advance Peter's denial (Matt. 26:34) and the treachery of Judas (John 13:18-19). He also foretold His own resurrection from the dead after three days (John 2:19), as well as the outpouring of the Holy Spirit following His departure (John 14:16-17), the persecution His followers would suffer (Matt. 10:16-22), the destruction of the Jerusalem temple (Matt. 24:2), and the complex of events associated with His second coming and the consummation of the age (Matt. 24:3-31).

Not only His words but also His deeds reflect the spirit of true prophecy. Our Lord's prophetic message was substantiated by the example of His prophetic life. John insists that in His very person Jesus made a prophetic declaration of God. "No man has seen God at any time; the only begotten God, who is in the bosom of the Father, He has explained Him" (John 1:18). Jesus, too, claimed that through the total impact of His life—His example and His actions, as well as His words—"I have manifested Thy name" (John 17:6).

Today Jesus' prophetic ministry continues through His Spirit-anointed followers. As the church proclaims God's Word (2 Cor. 5:19) and lives the exemplary life of our Lord (1 John 2:6), it exercises a prophetic ministry in the world. As Oswald J. Sanders says in *The Incomparable Christ,* "The church is a prophetic institution whose function it is to teach the world by its preaching and ordinances."

Christ's Priestly Office

If the prophet in Israel addressed the people in the name of God, the priest addressed God on behalf of the people. Hebrews virtually defines for us the ministry of a priest: "every high priest . . . is appointed on behalf of men in things pertaining to God in order to offer both gifts and sacrifices for sins" (Heb. 5:1). The Old Testament priest was the divinely appointed intermediary between sinful man and the holy God.

Several Old Testament intimations of Christ's priestly office lay the foundation for the fully developed teaching of Hebrews in the New Testament. Genesis introduces us to Melchizedek, the priest-king of Salem (Gen. 14:18). And in Exodus 28 and 29 we find the institution of the Aaronic priesthood during Israel's sojourn in the wilderness. Only the divinely ordained Aaronic priest could offer sacrifices and approach God in the inner chamber of the tabernacle. The Aaronic priesthood, however, with its repetitive animal sacrifices which could never remove sins (Heb. 10:4), could only point beyond itself to the perfect priesthood of Christ.

A more explicit reference to the messianic priest is found in Zechariah's prophecy uttered at the coronation of Joshua, the high priest. The prophet spoke of the "Branch" as one who "will build the temple of the Lord, and He who will bear the honor and sit and rule on His throne" (Zech. 6:12-13). Clearly, Zechariah envisioned the Messiah as both priest and king.

When we come to the New Testament we find that of all the New Testament books, Hebrews alone calls our Lord "priest." In its 12 uses of the term, the Epistle teaches that Christ had all the necessary qualifications for appointment to priestly office. He is able to represent us before God because He was fully human. He felt the tug of temptation; He knew the reality of suffering; He sensed the demand of total obedience to the Father (Heb. 5:7-8). Precisely because Christ fully shared our lot—sin alone excepted— "He is able to come to the aid of those who are tempted" (Heb. 2:18).

Hebrews shows, however, that Christ is priest of a radically new order foreshadowed by Melchizedek (Heb. 5:10; 6:20). The ancient priest-king of Salem, so the Epistle says, was superior to the patriarch Abraham, and hence to Levi who was yet in Abraham's "loins" (Heb 7:10): (1) Abraham paid tithes to Melchizedek (Heb. 7:4); (2) Melchizedek pronounced a blessing on the patriarch (Heb. 7:6-7); and (3) Melchizedek lives on, there being no record in Genesis of his death (Heb. 7:8).

Having established the superiority of Melchizedek's priesthood to that of Aaron, the writer proceeds to explain what is meant by priesthood "after the order of Melchizedek." (1) Melchizedek was a forerunner of the "king of righteousness" and "king of peace" who would unite in His person priesthood with royalty (Heb. 7:1-2); (2) he foreshadowed Christ in that his priesthood was established not on physical descent from any priestly regime, but solely upon his innate personal worth (Heb. 7:3a); and supremely, (3) Melchizedek was an earthly figure of the eternal Son of God who possesses neither beginning nor end of personal existence (Heb. 7:3b).

The writer also records several characteristics of the Melchizedekian High Priest which set Him above the priests of Aaron. Unlike the latter who needed to atone for their own sins, Jesus was a *sinless* high priest. Here is "One who has been tempted in all things as we are, yet without sin" (Heb. 4:15b). The moral character of the Christian's High Priest is incomparable. He is "holy, innocent, undefiled, separated from sinners" (Heb. 7:26). Christ, moreover, is a perfectly *empathetic* high priest. Because

He fully entered into the human situation, Christ actually suffers along with His distressed people (Heb. 4:15a).

Finally, our Lord is represented as an *exalted* priestly ministrant. Hebrews makes a claim for Christ which cannot be equalled. "We have a great high priest who has passed through the heavens" (Heb. 4:14). Having ascended to the right hand of God, Christ ministers in a sanctuary not made with hands (Heb. 9:24).

Hebrews makes the additional point that Christ's priesthood is superior to all rivals. This lofty claim is supported by three arguments. First, Christ's Melchizedekian priesthood is *unique*. Under the Aaronic system the high priestly office was occupied by a long line of ministrants. When one high priest died, another was appointed. But the Scripture says of Christ, "He holds His priesthood permanently, because He continues for ever" (Heb. 7:24, RSV). Christ neither assumed His priestly office from a predecessor, nor will He pass it on to any successor.

In addition, Christ's priesthood is fully *efficacious*. The blood of the Aaronic sacrifices removed only external ceremonial pollution (Heb. 10:4). But on the ground of His atoning sacrifices Christ is "able to save absolutely those who approach God through Him" (Heb. 7:25, NEB).

Another excellence of Christ's priesthood is that it is *eternal*. The Christian's High Priest acceded to office "by the power of an indestructible life" (Heb. 7:16). The unbounded eternity of Christ's priesthood is the single great theme of the seventh chapter of Hebrews (vv. 3, 17, 21, 25, 28). Without a doubt, Jesus is the great high priest *par excellence!*

Christ's Kingly Office

In ancient Near Eastern cultures the king wielded a wide range of powers—e.g., executive, legislative, judicial, fiscal, and military. Consequently the king exercised almost total authority over his subjects. In the case of Israel, God willed that He alone rule over His people as King. But when the nation clamored for an earthly monarch, Saul was chosen to ascend the throne.

When Saul failed in his royal task, David was secretly anointed Israel's ruler (1 Sam. 16:13). Nathan predicted that God would establish the throne of David's kingdom forever (2 Sam. 7:12-14). The kingdom attained the zenith of material prosperity and power during the rule of Solomon. Toward the end of Solomon's reign voluptuous living and spiritual declension tarnished the glory of the kingdom. During the rule of Solomon's sensuous son, Rehoboam, the kingdom tragically split in two. The corrupt kings who followed did little to prevent the collapse and subjugation of the divided kingdom by heathen powers. Following the exile, the loss of political freedom under the Persians, the guerrilla warfare and intrigue of the Maccabean era, and the oppressive rule of the Herods heightened Israel's yearning for a king who would restore forever the dignity and glory of the house of David.

Throughout Israel's checkered history songs of praise fanned the hope of a royal Messiah. Psalm 2:6-11 speaks of a day in which God's Son will rule with a rod of iron. Psalm 72 extols the majesty and glory of Solomon's reign. Yet the song transcends the historical moment in somber anticipation of the righteous rule of the Christ. And, finally, Psalm 110 depicts the Messiah as both a King and a Priest forever, a judgment confirmed by our Lord (Matt. 22:43-44), Peter (Acts 2:34), and the writer of Hebrews (Heb. 7:1ff.).

This hope of a royal Messiah intensified during the period of the writing prophets. Isaiah provided magnificent hints of the righteous and peaceful character of Christ's kingly reign (Isa. 2:1-4; 9:6-7; 11:1-10; 32:1; 33:17). Jeremiah spoke of the "righteous Branch" who "will reign as king and act wisely, and do justice and righteousness in the land" (Jer. 23:5). God gave Daniel a remarkable vision of the Son of man who would receive "dominion, glory, and a kingdom . . . which will not pass away" (Dan. 7:13-14). Ezekiel beheld the Messiah as a shepherd, prince, and king over the restored house of David (Ezek. 34:22-24; 37:24-25). For Micah Christ was the preexistent ruler of Israel (Micah 5:2). And Zechariah saw in the king who would enter Jerusalem on a colt (Zech. 9:9) the object of universal worship (14:16-17).

Aware of these prophecies, the New Testament writers were convinced that Jesus was the promised King. The angel Gabriel announced to Mary that at His birth her child would inherit the throne of His father David (Luke 1:32-33). And eastern astrologers, led by a star, inquired after the infant Jesus, "Where is He who has been born King of the Jews?" (Matt. 2:2) Later, John the Baptist, aware of God's rule in the person of the Nazarene, summoned the people to repentance with the words, "The kingdom of heaven is at hand" (Matt. 3:2).

Once, even Jesus Himself reminded an unbelieving crowd of the Queen of Sheba, who went to great trouble to investigate reports of the wisdom of Solomon. "Now," the Lord said, "one greater than Solomon is here" (Matt. 12:42, NIV).

In the present age, however, the kingdom, said Jesus, is spiritual rather than material, hidden rather than openly manifest. After He had excised various evil powers He said to the Pharisees, "If I cast out demons by the Spirit of God, then the kingdom of God has come upon you" (Matt. 12:28). The message of our Lord's miracles pointed unmistakably to His powerful rule in the world. That is why Jesus spoke of His authority over Satan to the 70 who had returned from their mission: "I was watching Satan fall from heaven like lightning" (Luke 10:18). The power of Christ's future rule had already shattered the dominion of Satan and his dark host. D-Day had arrived; V-Day lay just ahead. It would be a life-changing event.

Matthew's Gospel in particular speaks clearly of Jesus' spiritual rule. Prior to entering Jerusalem for the last time, Jesus declared that the prophecy of Zechariah 9:9 was about to be fulfilled: "Behold, your King is coming to you, gentle, and mounted upon a donkey" (Matt. 21:5). Similarly, when He taught about the return of the Son of man at the close of the age, He plainly referred to Himself as King (Matt. 25:34, 40). Later, during our Lord's final hours, His kingship was often in the foreground. Jesus made no attempt to deny the charge when the cowardly Pilate posed the question, "Are you the King of the Jews?" (Matt. 27:11). That helps to explain the events surrounding the Crucifixion. When Jesus was delivered at last to the executioners the Roman soldiers mocked and reviled Him: "Hail, King of the Jews!" (Matt. 27:29) Then through the city they drove Him with His cross and the charge against Him soon to be mounted over His head: "This is Jesus the King of the Jews" (Matt. 27:37).

This apparent weakness, that ultimately will result in power, lies behind Paul's claim that Christ now exercises kingly rule over the universe (Eph. 1:20-22) and that, after Satan's final overthrow, Christ will surrender His royal authority to the Father who first entrusted it to Him (1 Cor. 15:24).

The most graphic portrait of Jesus' kingly rule, however, appears in Revelation. There John acknowledges Jesus as the King who will occupy the throne of David (Rev. 3:7, 21; 5:5) and he teaches that the present world order will end with the coming of the "King of kings and Lord of lords" who will vanquish the enemies of God and rule with a rod of iron (19:11-16).

A noted theologian tells of a visit he once had with Mahatma Ghandi, the late Prime Minister of India. After a time the conversation turned to spiritual matters. The theologian tactfully related to Ghandi his own personal experience of the Lordship of Jesus Christ. Ghandi quietly pondered the Christian's testimony and then lamented, "My own throne is still vacant."

Who is a Christian but one who has crowned Jesus Christ Lord and King of his entire life? As someone has said, "He is not Lord at all until he is Lord of all."

Summing Up

As we have seen, then, Christ perfectly fulfilled and united in His person the three main strands of Old Testament messianic expectation. The Carpenter of Nazareth is first the Prophet who proclaims the Word of the Lord, then the Priest who abolishes sin by sacrifice and intercession, and finally the King who rules over the entire universe. This threefold scheme provides a picture of the mediatorial work which our Lord came to earth to accomplish.

Charles Hodge, the 19th-century Princeton theologian, aptly summarized Christ's relevance for the church as Prophet, Priest, and King when he wrote, "Fallen men, ignorant, guilty, polluted, and helpless, need a Saviour who is a prophet to instruct us; a priest to atone and make intercession for us; and a king to rule over and protect us."

10

Dying Saviour

One Sunday morning a minister preached a sermon on Christ's atoning death for sin. Following the service a man took issue with the preacher. "I don't believe a word that you said," complained the critic.

"You don't believe in the Atonement?" replied the minister.

"No, I don't!"

"Then, how is a person saved?"

After a few moments thought the skeptic answered, "I think we are saved by obeying the teachings of Jesus, by following His example and by doing His will; not by His death."

The Centrality of the Cross

This incident illustrates the division in Protestantism over the issue of the Cross. Liberals view Christ's death as the supreme example of perfect obedience and love for others. Evangelicals, on the other hand, insist that Christ died on the cross to make amends for the world's sin.

Scripture itself plainly teaches that the purpose of Christ's coming to earth was to die. The Cross was more than a tragic failure at the end of a successful career. It was the focal point of our Lord's earthly life. Everything else pointed to it. The disproportionate space in the Gospels allotted to the final week of Jesus' life confirms this. Matthew devotes 33 percent of his Gospel to the drama of Jesus' last few days, Mark 37 percent, Luke 25 percent, and John 42 percent. One scholar quite rightly speaks of the Gospel records as passion narratives with extended introductions. By way of striking contrast, the death of Martin Luther King shook the world, yet King's biographer devotes only 35 out of 362 pages to the last days of his life.

If God is love, however, why did God's blameless Son have to suffer and die? The Bible provides an answer to this difficult problem. Christ died because of our sinfulness (Rom. 5:8). He died because God's sentence for sin is death (Rom. 6:23).

Chrysostom, the early church father, was once persecuted because he refused to violate his conscience and the Word of God. The Roman Empress threatened Chrysostom with more severe punishment if he continued to criticize her. The saintly Christian ordered a runner to relay to the Empress this message: "Go tell her that I fear nothing but sin."

The Bible paints a grim picture of sin. It is a horrible disease, a huge debt, a horrendous load. Christ's suffering and death make sense only against the backdrop of the seriousness of sin. Far from an injustice, the Cross, said J. H. Jowett, is "the last pregnant syllable of God's great utterance of love."

Examining the Record

W. H. Griffith Thomas once said that "in a very real sense Calvary began in the Garden." He was right. The significance of the Cross is captured only by considering the web of events leading up to that fatal hour. Just hours before Gethsemane the chief priests and elders plotted together in the palace of Caiaphas to kill Jesus (Matt. 26:3-5). Perhaps disillusioned with the apparent failure of Jesus' political program, Judas joined the budding conspiracy (Matt. 26:14-16). So for 30 pieces of silver—the value of a common slave (Ex. 21:32)—Judas consented to deliver up the Lord to the Jewish authorities.

About midnight Jesus and the Eleven rose from Supper (Matt. 26:30-35) and crossed the brook Kedron to the Garden of Gethsemane. There in that favorite place of prayer Jesus faced the mounting crisis head-on (Matt. 26:36-46). He took Peter, James, and John further into the Garden, but eventually left even them that He might meet with God alone.

As Jesus wrestled with His destiny an intense spiritual battle raged. The Gospels relate that Jesus became "very distressed and troubled" (Mark 14:33). The One who was always "a Man of sorrows" became "deeply grieved, even to the point of death" (Matt. 26:38). As Jesus agonized over "the cup"—the experience God had assigned Him—His sweat became like great drops of blood (Luke 22:44).

What was in the vial which caused our Lord to pray, "remove this cup from Me"? (Luke 22:42) Perhaps three things: (1) the concerted attacks of the powers of darkness (Luke 22:53); (2) the guilt of a sinful world (Isa. 53:6); and (3) the wrath of an offended God (Rom. 1:18). But despite the horrors of the cup Jesus pursued the path of obedience. He said, "Yet not My will, but Thine be done" (Luke 22:42).

Scarcely had Jesus returned to His sleeping disciples when a raucous mob armed with swords and clubs and led by Judas entered the Garden (Matt. 26:47-56). According to plan the traitor was to give Jesus the customary kiss of greeting. But Matthew and Mark relate that Judas embraced Jesus and kissed Him fervently. A single kiss from the traitor was evil enough. But as it was, shame was heaped upon shame!

In the early hours of the next morning Jesus was led, bound, to Annas, the ex-high priest, while the Sanhedrin hastily gathered at the palace of Caiaphas (John 18:12-24). The Jewish Talmud reflects the low esteem the people had of this priestly bureaucracy in Jerusalem. "Woe to the family of Annas! Woe to their serpent-like kisses!" Jesus was tried then before an irregular night session of the Sanhedrin presided over by Caiaphas, son-in-law of Annas (Luke 22:54, 63-65). Far from safeguarding the rights of the accused, the Sanhedrin turned a blind eye while the temple police mocked, beat, and spat upon the guiltless Jesus.

At first light Jesus was brought back before the Sanhedrin in a vain attempt to legitimize the proceedings (Matt. 26:59-68). The Jews knew they had no case against Jesus so they brought false witnesses to testify to trumped-up charges. Jesus eloquently answered the wild charges with unbroken silence.

Finally, the high priest placed Jesus under an oath and demanded to know whether or not He was the Son of God. Jesus openly confessed He was the Messiah, whereupon Caiaphas furiously tore off his mantle while hurling at the Lord charges of blasphemy.

Jesus' trials before the Jewish authorities were riddled with prejudice, fraud, and illegality. According to Jewish oral law, capital cases could not be tried at night. Jesus was. Some of His judges (members of the Sanhedrin) even participated in Jesus' arrest. Trials were supposed to be conducted in public, but all three of Jesus' trials were held in secret. Moreover, the chief witnesses who spoke against Jesus had been bribed. Finally, the requirement that at least 24 hours must elapse between trial and sentencing was overlooked. So irregular were the ecclesiastical trials that it is clear Jesus' death was determined even before the court convened.

Since the Jews were not permitted to levy the death sentence (John 18:31), Jesus was led away to Pilate, the Roman Procurator over Judea (Matt. 27:11-14). After weighing the charges brought by the Jews, Pilate concluded, "I find no guilt in this man" (Luke 23:4). Hoping to rid himself of a difficult situation, Pilate sent Jesus to Herod Antipas, Tetrarch of Galilee (Luke 23:8-12). The cunning king, whom Jesus referred to as "that fox" (Luke 13:32), had little interest in Jesus' fate. He wanted only to be entertained.

So back to the Romans Jesus went, His fate once again resting in Pilate's hands (Matt. 27:15-26). Convinced that the Galilean was innocent of all charges, Pilate hoped that the crowd would consent to His release. But the people wanted only Jesus' blood. Thus, the weak-willed Pilate washed his hands of the matter and handed over Jesus to the Jews to be crucified.

Every Easter we rehearse the drama of the crucifixion (Matt. 27:32-50). Bruised and lacerated, Jesus bore the weight of the Roman cross up the Via Dolorosa, until aided by Simon of Cyrene. The record is stark in its simplicity. "When they came to the place which is called The Skull, there they crucified Him" (Luke 23:33).

Crucifixion was a shameful form of execution reserved for slaves and the worst criminals. It was also one of the cruelest in the ancient world. Seven-inch spikes were hammered through wrists and feet. So the Lord was nailed to a tree between two guilty thieves. The Roman soldiers assigned to the scene entertained themselves by stripping Jesus and gambling for His garments (Matt. 27:35). Such humiliation added to the mockery of the inscription fixed over His head: "Jesus the Nazarene, the King of the Jews" (John 19:19). The Passover pilgrims who paraded by joined the thieves on either side of Jesus in railing at Him (Matt. 27:39, 44).

For six agonizing hours the Lord hung on the cross, His clothing stripped from His body, His flesh torn and bleeding, each breath causing excruciating pain. Crucifixion meant intense physical suffering. But the Lord suffered even more in spirit as the sins of the world were heaped on Him.

In the art galleries of Europe there is a painting of the crucifixion by Matthias Grunewald. It depicts John the Baptist with an unnaturally elongated finger pointing to the Crucified. The painting is a parable. The finger of all of human history points to the One who bore the sins of the world on Golgotha.

For three hours, beginning at noon, a strange darkness settled over the land. The light of the sun failed as God made His Son to be sin for us (2 Cor. 5:21). Suddenly an anguished cry from Jesus' lips pierced the darkness: "My God, My God, why hast Thou forsaken me?" (Matt. 27:46) As the Almighty turned His back on the Son, Jesus could not utter the words, "My Father." Thinking Jesus was calling for Elijah, an observer filled a sponge with cheap vinegar wine and put it to Jesus' mouth in an attempt to quench His thirst.

Finally, after six hours of excruciating agony, Jesus uttered one final cry—"It is finished!"—then surrendered up His life (John 19:30). In the original, the cry "It is finished!" is a single word. In the ancient world the artist would speak the word after putting the final touches on his painting. The Lamb of God offered Himself as a sacrifice on the altar of the Cross, and when the task of redemption was completed, the Saviour of the world cried out

"Finished!" and breathed His last. With the offering of this sacrifice, the veil to the temple Holy of Holies was torn from top to bottom. The way into the presence of God was now opened to all who would come (Heb. 9:7-8; 10:19-22).

The Death of Christ in Scripture

This sacrificial death of Jesus Christ is the central theme of the Word of God. In his book *What the Bible Teaches,* R. A. Torrey estimates that there are over 333 references to the death of Christ in the Old Testament and more than 175 in the New. In the Old Testament sacrificial system, which pointed to the perfect sacrifice of Christ, the Aaronic priest took an unblemished animal, placed his hands on the sacrifice to symbolize the transfer of Israel's guilt to the victim, killed the animal, and sprinkled its blood before the altar. This common practice provided the background for the New Testament writers' references to Christ's death as the fulfillment of the Mosaic sacrificial ritual (Eph. 5:2; 1 Peter 1:2).

Later in Old Testament history the musicians and prophets of Israel anticipated the suffering and death of the Lord's Anointed. Although written a thousand years before Jesus' birth, Psalm 22 presents an incredibly vivid picture of the suffering Saviour. Of course, Isaiah 52:13—53:12 offers the most detailed prophetic picture of our Lord's passion. In his widely used *Handbook,* Halley says that prophecy is "so vivid in detail that one would almost think of Isaiah as standing at the foot of the cross." The prophet Zechariah might have joined him since his remarkable portrait includes the Lord's betrayal (Zech. 11:12), scourging (13:7), atoning death (3:8-9; 13:1), and reign as priest and king (6:13).

For the New Testament writers, the focus of Jesus' life was His death. John the Baptist's annunciation of Jesus' ministry was right to the point. "Behold, the Lamb of God who takes away the sin of the world" (John 1:29).

While Jesus did not come to talk about His death, but to die, He did try to prepare His disciples for the inevitable. At the outset of His ministry He told the Jews, "Destroy this temple, and in three days I will raise it up" (John 1:29); and later He claimed, "I am the living bread . . . and the bread also which I shall give for the life of the world is My flesh" (John 6:51). After Peter's confession at Caesarea Philippi, Jesus spoke to His disciples openly about the necessity of the Cross. He "began to show His disciples that He must go to Jerusalem, and suffer many things from the elders and chief priests and scribes, and be killed" (Matt. 16:21). Later, enroute to Jerusalem (Matt. 20:19), the Lord reminded His disciples a number of times that He must be betrayed and delivered up to a cruel death.

Certainly, in its missionary preaching, the early church faithfully proclaimed Christ's death. The Cross was central in the messages of Peter (Acts 2:23; 3:15) and Stephen (Acts 7:52) even before Paul reminded the Corinthians that "I delivered to you as of first importance . . . that Christ died for our sins" (1 Cor. 15:3). The point is clear: in its preaching, teaching, and hymns the early church assigned to Christ's death a position of central importance.

The Significance of Christ's Death

What was it, however, that was accomplished as Christ hung on that Roman cross? Some believe that Jesus was crucified as a political criminal. He tried to launch a revolution, failed, and got what He deserved. Others suggest that Jesus died the death of a martyr. Here was a man who paid the ultimate price for His convictions. Still others believe that Jesus' death was intended as a model for sacrificial living.

At King's College in Cambridge, J. A. T. Robinson, the radical English churchman, gave a series of lectures on the person of Jesus Christ. At the close of the highly philosophical presentation, a student rose to address the speaker. "I'm an English major, not a theologian. Please explain in layman's terms what the Cross of Christ should mean to me."

The theologian replied, "Suppose you have been totally crushed by life and find yourself lying on your face in the mud. In the moment of deepest need you remember the crucified Jesus. As you think of Him something wonderful happens. Your heart is warmed and you find the courage to rise up from the mud to one knee."

A believing student in the audience couldn't remain silent. He rose to his feet and declared, "When I met the crucified Christ He gave me the power to stand up straight on two feet." The point is that for Bishop Robinson the value of Christ's death was a mere moral example.

The Word of God appears to endorse no single theory of the Atonement. Instead, it presents a series of word pictures to describe the rich and varied significance of our Lord's death.

For a start, Scripture represents Christ's passion as a *ransom*. In the Old Testament a ransom was the price paid to secure a slave's release (Isa. 45:13). Thus Christ's death somehow may be likened to the price paid to obtain the sinner's release from the slavery of sin and death (Matt. 20:28; 1 Tim. 2:6).

Christ's death is also represented as a *redemption*. The idea here is the slave's release from bondage (Ex. 21:8). Thus the Apostles taught that Christ's blood shed on the cross effectively secures our release from the domain of Satan (Eph. 1:7; 1 Peter 1:18-19).

Moreover, His death is presented as a *propitiation*. In pagan Greek literature the word was used of an offering which would placate the angry gods. It is rendered "propitiation" in Romans 3:25; 1 John 2:2; and 4:10 and translated "mercy seat" in Hebrews 9:5. The background of this last use is a key to the term's meaning. In the Old Testament the mercy seat, in the Holy of Holies, was the place where the blood of the sacrifice was sprinkled. As a result of the blood God's wrath was appeased. Similarly, the blood-sprinkled body of Christ became for all time the "mercy seat" for sinners. Through Christ's death on the cross, all the demands of a holy and just God were satisfied. The divine anger was turned into kindly favor.

The word *reconciliation* further describes the potency of the Cross. Paul wrote: "We rejoice in God through our Lord Jesus Christ, through whom we have now received our reconciliation" (Rom. 5:11, NIV; see also Rom. 11:15; 2 Cor. 5:18-19). The King James Version renders the term "atonement." The word was first coined by William Tyndale, the English Reformer, who conceived of Christ's work on the cross as an act of "at-one-ment." God and man were estranged due to sin. But because of the satisfaction wrought by Christ, God justly restores repentent sinners to full fellowship with Himself.

Christ's work on the cross is also represented as a *substitutionary sacrifice*. The idea here is that Christ took on Himself the sinner's guilt and bore its penalty in the sinner's place. Isaiah saw mankind as wayward and sinful. Yet "the Lord had laid on Him the iniquity of us all" (Isa. 53:6). In a similar way Peter saw the Atonement as a substitutionary act: "He Himself bore our sins in His body on the cross . . . by His wounds you were healed" (1 Peter 2:24, see also 3:18).

Luther spoke in glowing terms of Christ's substitutionary work. "This is the mystery of the riches of divine grace for sinners," he said, "for by a wonderful exchange our sins are not ours but Christ's, and Christ's righteousness is not Christ's but ours."

Another believer from another age, J. P. Morgan, the wealthy banker, wrote these marvelous words in his will: "I commit my soul into the hands of my Saviour full of confidence that having received me and washed me with His precious blood He will present me spotless before the throne of my heavenly Father." All of his millions could not get Morgan into heaven; only Christ's cleansing blood could do that.

The Power of the Cross

Let's now summarize the saving benefits of Christ's death on Calvary. The most immediate effect, of course, is upon the believer who has bowed at the foot of the Cross. The Word teaches that whoever trusts in the dying Saviour is justified by God. *Justification* is a legal term signifying that God reckons the believer perfectly guiltless. God declares the trusting sinner righteous, because Christ bore the penalty due us, God's justice was satisfied. Paul then could say, "the free gift arose from many transgressions resulting in justification" (Rom. 5:16; see also 3:24).

Luther, who preached justification by faith alone into the heart of the Reformation, once said, "Nothing more is required for justification than to hear of Jesus Christ and to believe on Him as our Saviour."

Second, Scripture teaches that by the Cross the world was reconciled unto God. John the Baptist proclaimed at the outset of Jesus' ministry, "Behold the Lamb of God who takes away the sin of the world!" (John 1:29) And Paul wrote: "God was in Christ reconciling the world to Himself" (2 Cor. 5:19).

Neither John nor Paul, however, taught a crass universalism. These texts do not imply that every person will be converted. What Scripture means is that Christ's atonement has removed every obstacle to salvation except willful resistance to the Gospel. As Matthew Henry put it, the Atonement "is sufficient for all, but effectual for many."

The death of Christ likewise had an effect upon Satan. The power of "the ruler of this world" was curbed by the Lamb who hung on the tree (John 12:31). Satan is a defeated foe. The believer need not fear his terror. "Having drawn the sting of all the powers ranged against us," the Apostle Paul wrote, "[Jesus] exposed them, shattered, empty, and defeated, in His final glorious triumphant act!" (Col. 2:15, PH)

Furthermore, the Cross of Christ had a profound effect upon the universe as a whole. Paul declares that God was pleased "to reconcile *all things* to Himself, having made peace by the blood of His cross" (Col. 1:20). Through sin the cosmos became a chaos— defiled, fragmented, and shattered. But Christ's atonement somehow touched the entire created order. The Cross works to undo the effects of the Fall and to restore the beauty, order, and design of the original creation. One day the redemption of the physical universe will be completed (Rom. 8:21).

Finally, the cross upon which Christ secured our salvation casts its shadow over the church. If on one side of the coin is stamped Jesus' cross, on the other side is stamped our own. The former is meaningless without the latter. Our Lord Himself declared, "If anyone wishes to come after Me, let him deny himself, and take up his cross daily, and follow Me" (Luke 9:23). Thomas a Kempis said something of his own generation which we would do well to ponder. "Jesus has many lovers of His heavenly kingdom, but few bearers of His cross."

11

Resurrected Lord

Throughout the centuries men have tried to honor their heroes by erecting lavish monuments: the massive pyramids of Egypt, built as resting places for the Egyptian pharaohs; the glistening Taj Mahal, the tomb of an Indian emperor and his favorite wife; Lenin's Tomb in Red Square, the place where the body of the Marxist leader is preserved by some mysterious process; the burial vault at Mt. Vernon, the site of President Washington's interred body.

In its stark simplicity Jesus' grave can't compare with these costly crypts. But the tomb of Jesus excels in the most important respect. It lies empty! He is not there!

At the heart of the Christian faith is the claim that Jesus Christ on the third day rose from the dead and is alive forevermore. The Apostles' Creed confesses in simple words, "I believe in Jesus Christ . . . who . . . the third day rose from the dead." No other world religion has dared to make such a confession—be it Buddhism, Confucianism, Islam, or Mormonism.

For a century now Americans have studied "comparative religions." But there is nothing "comparative" about Christianity. It is the superlative religion because of the resurrection of Jesus from the grave. The religions of the world evoke an air of death. Only the Christian faith affirms life, hope, and immortality.

In John Masefield's drama *The Trial of Jesus,* Procula, the wife

113

of Pilate, receives a report that Jesus rose from the tomb. She excitedly asks Longinus, a Roman soldier, "Do you think He is dead?"

"No, I don't," Longinus replies.

"Where then is He?" Procula asks.

"Loose in the world, lady," says Longinus, "where neither Jew nor Roman nor anyone else can stop Him!" This is the heartbeat of Christianity.

Scripture and the Resurrection

Before He returned to heaven, Jesus claimed that His death and resurrection were foretold in the Old Testament (Luke 24:25-27, 44-46). The Apostle Paul also declared that Christ both died and rose again in direct fulfillment of prophetic Scripture (1 Cor. 15:4).

The Old Testament Scriptures, in the main, celebrated the glory of the here and now. To be blessed of God was to live a long and productive life. For this reason the resurrection of the body was not widely taught in the Old Testament.

Nevertheless, several clear intimations of Christ's resurrection from the dead were given hundreds of years before the event. Job's confession surely anticipated our Lord's rising. "I know that my Redeemer lives, and at the last He will take His stand on the earth" (Job 19:25). David, also, inspired by the Spirit, could say, "Thou wilt make known to me the path of life; in Thy presence is fulness of joy; in Thy right hand there are pleasures forever" (Ps. 16:11). We know this prophecy was not totally fulfilled in David's experience because Peter (Acts 2:25-28) and Paul (Acts 13:35-37) clearly testify that David was speaking of Christ who had yet to come.

The prophet Isaiah added his witness to this testimony when he wrote: "He will swallow up death for all time" (Isa. 25:8). And the prophecy of Hosea (6:2) most certainly adds a further prediction of our Lord's resurrection. As Barnes notes in his commentary, "The prophet expressly mentions *two days,* after which life would be given, and a *third day,* on which the resurrection should take place. What else can this be than the two days in which the body of Christ lay in the tomb, and the third day, on which He rose again?"

The New Testament builds on this teaching with six independent accounts of Christ's resurrection—the four Gospels, Acts, and the Pauline Letters. In the Gospels, Jesus rarely spoke of His impending death without mention of His resurrection three days later. At the outset of His public ministry the Lord said to the Jews, "Destroy this temple, and in three days I will raise it up" (John 2:19). It was clear to John that Jesus spoke of His own body (John 2:21). Later, the Lord used the story of Jonah's three days in the belly of a whale to foretell His own death and resurrection (Matt. 12:40).

After Peter's confession near Caesarea Philippi (Matt. 16:21) Jesus made specific predictions of His resurrection. He made the point so often that even the chief priests and Pharisees got wind of it and told Pilate that Jesus claimed He would rise after three days (Matt. 27:63).

For good reasons, then, the Evangelists made the resurrection of Christ the climax and conclusion of their narratives. Each of the Gospels portrays the web of events surrounding our Lord's ascent from the grave (Matt. 28:1-20; Mark 16:1-8; Luke 24:1-53; John 20:1-21, 25). Their accounts of the empty tomb, the Lord's appearances in bodily form, His exhortations to the disciples, and His ascension to heaven all bear the marks of carefully researched historical records. One cannot escape the conviction that Christ's resurrection stands as the crowning miracle of God's revelation to man. J. S. Whale is correct in declaring that "the Gospels do not explain the Resurrection; the Resurrection explains the Gospels."

Naturally, then, the empty tomb was the theme of the early church's missionary preaching. In his sermon at Pentecost, Peter dwelt extensively on the reality and significance of God's act of raising Jesus from the dead. Because the resurrection so clearly attests God's endorsement of Jesus' message and mission, Christian preaching in Acts stressed the Resurrection even more than the Cross. Peter's second sermon (Acts 3:15), the expanding witness of the Jerusalem church (Acts 4:33; 5:31), Peter's testimony to Cornelius (Acts 10:40-42), Paul's preaching at Antioch (Acts

13:30-37) and Athens (Acts 17:18, 31), and his defense before King Agrippa (Acts 26:23) all stressed the implications of Christ's resurrection from the dead. All this explains Andrew Blackwood's observation: "There is not a single pessimistic note anywhere in the New Testament after the resurrection."

The Book of Acts explains also the life and mission of the Apostle to the Gentiles. Paul, who was then called Saul, was an up-and-coming rabbi. He was a bright young intellectual who sat under the famous Gamaliel at the rabbinical academy in Jerusalem. So hostile was Saul to the Christian movement that he became its leading persecutor.

Yet after Saul met the risen Lord on the road to Damascus he proclaimed Christ and the Resurrection with the utmost zeal. Writing to the church at Thessalonica in about A.D. 51, Paul could say, "We believe that Jesus died and rose again" (1 Thes. 4:14). To the Corinthians, who held that "dead men don't rise," Paul wrote, "I delivered to you as of first importance what I also received, that Christ . . . was raised on the third day according to the Scriptures" (1 Cor. 15:3-4). B. F. Westcott, the late 19th-century Cambridge professor, summed it up well when he said, the Resurrection "is not an accessory of the apostolic message, but the sum of the message itself."

Suppose He Never Rose

As we have noted, Jesus predicted He would rise from the grave on the third day and the Apostles testified that the Resurrection did occur. But suppose Jesus and His followers could be proved wrong. Suppose Easter never happened. What then?

First of all, if Jesus never rose, His credibility as a teacher would be seriously compromised. If Christ's teaching about His own resurrection proved false, why should we regard as authoritative His other teachings about God, man, sin, and judgment?

Certainly, Christ's claim to deity would be impugned if Easter never occurred. Paul states that Jesus was "declared with power to be the Son of God . . . by the resurrection from the dead" (Rom. 1:4). If Jesus never rose we would have no right to esteem Him anything more than a mere man. The most convincing apologetic for Christ's true Godhead is the fact that He did, in truth, rise from the grave.

If Jesus remained in the tomb we would be forced to stamp the Gospel "null and void." Without Easter the Cross is reduced to a tragedy. So Paul argues in his great Resurrection chapter: "If Christ has not been raised, your faith is worthless; you are still in your sins" (1 Cor. 15:17). No Resurrection, no remission of sins, and no redemption. That being the case, Christians might as well "eat and drink, for tomorrow we die" (1 Cor. 15:32). But Paul is certain beyond a doubt that Christ "was raised because of our justification" (Rom. 4:25).

J. Sidlow Baxter tells of a rumor which swept across Asia to the effect that the bones of Buddha had been discovered. The reputed bones were paraded through the streets of India where millions gave homage. A Christian missionary watched the people prostrate themselves before the bones. Then he said to a friend, "If one bone of Jesus Christ were found, Christianity would fall to pieces." He was right.

If Christ did not rise from the dead there would be no resurrection life in the Spirit. Scripture makes the astonishing claim that the believer, spiritually united with the risen Christ, participates in the reality and power of his Lord's resurrection life (Rom. 6:4-5). In a real sense God sees believers as risen with Christ (Col. 3:1) and seated in heavenly places in Him (Eph. 2:5-6).

A Scotsman was once asked if he ever expected to go to heaven. His immediate reply was, "Why, mon, I live there!" He entered heaven before leaving this body because he possessed the reality of Christ's resurrection life.

Finally, if Christ did not rise bodily from the tomb, the Christian's hope of a future resurrection would be an illusion. If the Lord's body decayed in the tomb, His followers likewise would remain bound by the power of death. And if that be so, "we are of all men most to be pitied" (1 Cor. 15:19).

But since God *has* raised His Son, the believer confidently anticipates the resurrection of his own body. As Paul declared, "He who raised the Lord Jesus will raise us also with Jesus" (2 Cor. 4:14). D. L. Moody once said, "Someday you will read in the paper that D. L. Moody is dead. Don't you believe a word of it. At that moment I shall be more alive than I am now. That which is born of the Spirit will live forever."

The Saviour's Resurrection Body

Since the Bible teaches that the believer's own future body will be patterned after Christ's glorified body (Phil. 3:21), most Christians are interested in the character of our Lord's resurrection body. The exact nature of this body, however, is not explicitly stated in Scripture. Nevertheless, certain inferences can be drawn from hints here and there.

Of first importance is the fact that Jesus was raised with a physical body. When Paul preached the bodily resurrection of Christ at Athens, many mocked his message (Acts 17:32). The Greek Platonists believed that at death the spirit is set free while the body rots in the grave. Modernists also deny that Christ rose physically from the grave. Likewise, the Rev. Sun Myung Moon preaches a gospel which claims that Jesus did not rise bodily from the dead. According to Mr. Moon, Jesus came to save both spiritually and physically, but He failed and "left salvation on the physical level unaccomplished." But Scripture teaches that Christ redeemed the whole man, spirit and body. And our Lord rose bodily to validate this reality.

We note further that Jesus' resurrection body possessed a certain continuity with the body of His humiliation. Our Lord invited His perplexed disciples to observe the nail marks in His hands and feet (Luke 24:39) and the spear wound in His side (John 20:27). In addition, the resurrected Lord ate food (Luke 24:42-43), although it is unlikely that physical nourishment was required to sustain His life. On several occasions the disciples also readily recognized the risen One (Matt. 28:9; John 20:20).

On the other hand, Jesus' resurrection body possessed a certain discontinuity with His former body. The Lord suddenly appeared in the midst of His followers who had gathered behind locked doors (John 20:26). On another occasion He miraculously vanished before their eyes (Luke 24:31). At times even His closest friends did not immediately recognize Him (John 21:4).

In the light of these facts W. H. Griffith Thomas concludes that Christ's resurrection body was "the same though different, different though the same." It was a revealed mystery which we finite creatures cannot fully comprehend. It seems certain, though, that the resurrected Lord occupied the material body in which He suffered. But a radical change occurred at the Resurrection, whereby the Spirit of God animated the body of Jesus as its life-giving force. Thus Paul could describe the resurrection body of our Lord as a "heavenly body" (1 Cor. 15:40), a "spiritual body" (1 Cor. 15:44), and a "glorious body" (Phil. 3:21, KJV).

Silencing the Critics

Skeptics have challenged Christ's resurrection with persistent criticism. We want to outline now four leading arguments which have been advanced to counter belief in the Resurrection.

Some skeptics argue that Jesus never did die. The racking pain caused Him to fall into a state of unconsciousness. In the coolness of the tomb Jesus revived and His wounds began to heal. In fact, Jesus regained sufficient strength to roll back the stone and walk out of the cave.

This theory, however, overlooks several important facts. The Gospels record Jesus' dying gasp of breath on the cross. A spear was thrust in His side, which would have killed a man in so weak a condition. So certain were the Roman soldiers that He was dead, they did not bother to break His legs. Moreover, Joseph of Arimathea embalmed the dead body, and an armed Roman guard kept careful watch over the tomb. The "Swoon" Theory thus proved highly improbable.

Others assert that those who claimed to have seen Jesus were misled by strange visions or hallucinations. As a result of the heavy emotional strain of the long ordeal, Jesus' friends suffered extensive psychic disturbances. In a state of depression they saw what they *wanted* to see—a revived Jesus! One skeptic suggests that Mary Magdalene, who "saw" the angel before the empty tomb, suffered from hysterics to the verge of madness. So the critic argues: "Divine power of love! Sacred moments in which the passion of one possessed gave to the world a resuscitated god!"

This proposal, too, fails to satisfy. When Jesus died the disciples were thoroughly discouraged. They were certain that the end had come. Never again would they see Jesus. In resignation they returned to their fishing. There is simply no evidence that they were expecting a Resurrection.

Still other skeptics claim that the Resurrection was a tall tale fabricated by Jesus' friends. The story of Jesus' rising from the dead was the disciples' way of perpetuating His memory forever.

But this objection to the Resurrection also fails to square with the facts. The courageous life and heroic witness of the disciples prove that they were not "living a lie." Time and time again the Lord's followers staked their lives on the confidence that Jesus had, in fact, come alive.

Many liberals claim that the Resurrection belongs in the category of a myth. The "dying and rising god" motif of the pagan mystery religions infiltrated the Christian message, they say, giving birth to the myth of the Resurrection. Nevertheless, the myth itself conveys great religious truth. According to one critic, it teaches that "the activity of Jesus goes on."

This mythical interpretation, however, like all the others rests on a bias against the supernatural. Whatever contradicts the fixed laws of science must be unreal. So one prominent critic brashly concludes that "a resurrection from the dead is utterly inconceivable."

But the biblical Christian asserts that the resurrection of Jesus is an altogether reasonable belief. In fact, as we examine the evidence, the Resurrection proves to be the only consistent explanation of the remarkable events which occurred nearly 2,000 years ago.

First, there is the phenomenon of the empty tomb. Clearly the Jews didn't steal Jesus' body, for if they possessed the body, they only had to produce it to prove the Christian preaching false. It is also quite unlikely that the disciples removed the body. The frightened band of followers fled when Jesus was arrested. Who were 11 timid men in the face of a reinforced Roman guard?

Furthermore, the manner in which the graveclothes were rolled up separately and left in the grave demands some explanation.

When thieves ransack a house do they take the time to return everything neatly in place? Hardly.

Second, one must reckon with the collective force of the witnesses to Jesus' resurrection. The Christian claim does not rest on the testimony of a single distraught woman who in the morning's first light mistook a gardener for the risen Lord. No, over a period of 40 days, on 10 different occasions, as recorded by six ancient sources (the Gospels, Acts, and Pauline Epistles), Jesus appeared alive, sometimes to one or two individuals but on another occasion to 500 people. We can only conclude with one reputable scholar that "the original eye-witnesses were satisfied with the fact. Christ had appeared to them and was therefore risen."

Unbelief must also account for the disciples' radical transformation from fear and hesitation to extraordinary courage and boldness. We have seen that when Jesus died on the cross, the disciples' hopes died too. They all fled in fear. And most remained in hiding. Peter and a few of the others returned to their old life of fishing (John 21:2-3).

Yet within a short while we find the once-dispirited disciples glowing with confidence, and preaching Jesus and the Resurrection with great power. Not even the threat of death itself could silence their message. Only the reality of Christ's mighty resurrection could account for so revolutionary a change in so short a time. As the American jurist, Simon Greenleaf wrote in *A Treatise on the Law of Evidence,* "It was impossible that the disciples could have persisted in affirming the truth of the Resurrection had not Jesus actually risen from the dead."

The silence of Jesus' foes when faced with apostolic preaching of the Resurrection is further evidence of its truthfulness. Had opponents of the Gospel facts to disprove the Resurrection and thus silence the troublesome Christian movement, they would not have concealed them. Someone has said, "The silence of the Jews is as significant as the speech of the Christians."

Finally, opponents of the Resurrection must account for the rapid expansion of the Christian movement from a tiny band in Jerusalem to a mighty worldwide force. No ideology spread as rapidly in the ancient world as did Christianity. Persecution could not halt it. Although satanic error often parodies God's truth, the only adequate explanation of the church of Jesus Christ around the world is the resurrection of its Lord from the dead.

The Resurrection cannot be absolutely proven, as one proves a mathematical theorem. Beyond hard evidence, a reasonable step of faith must be taken. Yet the evidence compels us to conclude with Thomas Arnold of Rugby, that Christ's resurrection is the "best attested fact in human history." B. F. Westcott, in his book, *The Gospel of the Resurrection,* puts it this way. "It is not too much to say that there is no single historic incident better or more variously supported than the resurrection of Christ."

In one of the darkest hours of the Reformation, Martin Luther in a surge of emotion seized a crayon and wrote on the floor and paneling of his room, "The Lord lives! The Lord lives!" Without any doubt, Jesus' resurrection is the supreme victory. It represents the perfect climax to our Lord's pure and perfect life. It vindicates His claim to be the Son of God, and guarantees the believer's resurrection to eternal life in God's presence.

Its Significance for Us

Opponents of the Gospel say with Renan, the old French skeptic, "You Christians live on the fragrance of an empty vase." Our needy world invites the Christian to show by a transformed life of holiness, love, and power that the vase of our faith is not empty. One thinks of the unnumbered Christian martyrs who, in the confidence of resurrection victory, went to the lions singing in the Roman Colosseum. Or recent missionaries and other believers who have courageously laid down their lives in Ecuador, Viet Nam, or Uganda. Our privilege is to join them in "abnormal" Christianity, for God wills that He be glorified through the reality of the risen Lord living powerfully in and through His blood-bought people.

12

Seated Sovereign

In the Apostles' Creed Christians confess that Christ "on the third day rose again from the dead, ascended to heaven, sits on the right hand of God the Father almighty, thence He will come to judge the living and the dead." By so exalting the humiliated One, God brought His Son full circle: from glory to shame, back again to the glory and majesty of heaven.

This vision of coming glory originated with Jesus Himself. During His earthly ministry He predicted not only that He would suffer and die, but also that He would be exalted by divine power to heavenly dominion and splendor (John 17:5; Luke 24:26). He compared His life of humiliation to a grain of wheat which falls on the earth and dies (John 12:24). And He also spoke of His soon-coming exaltation to heaven: "The hour has come for the Son of Man to be glorified" (John 12:23). In this chapter we want to look more closely at the several stages of our Lord's exaltation, beginning with the Ascension.

Ascension to Glory
By the Ascension we mean the elevation of the God-man to heavenly splendor 40 days after His resurrection. It is one of the four great redemptive moments in the experience of the Saviour, that is, His incarnation, resurrection, ascension, and second com-

ing. J. G. Davies rightly claims that "the Ascension belongs not to the periphery, but to the heart and substance of the Gospel." The church, however, has paid insufficient attention to this event in its preaching and teaching.

When He ministered among men, our Lord often looked ahead to His ascension to the Father. For example, Jesus spoke of "the Son of Man ascending where He was before" (John 6:62). In the Upper Room He said to the Twelve, "Now I am going to Him who sent Me" (John 16:5). And on Easter morning the risen Christ appeared to Mary and charged her to tell the Disciples, "I ascend to My Father and your Father, and My God and your God" (John 20:17).

The event itself is recorded three times in the New Testament (Mark 16:19; Luke 24:51; Acts 1:9-11). Forty days after the empty tomb, while in the vicinity of Bethany, Jesus was caught up into a cloud and disappeared from sight. The disciples who witnessed His departure to heaven returned to Jerusalem to wait for the promised outpouring of the Holy Spirit.

Some might ask why Jesus waited nearly six weeks after the Resurrection before ascending to the Father. The answer is supplied in Acts 1:3. First, Jesus tarried long enough to restore the disciples' shattered faith through numerous personal appearances. Second, Jesus used the time to unfold to His followers the significance of the things He taught them while in the flesh. Luke relates that "beginning with Moses and with all the prophets, He explained to them the things concerning Himself in all the Scriptures (Luke 24:27; see also vv. 32, 44-47). Only after the risen Lord had renewed His followers' faith and enlightened their minds did He return to the Father and send the promised Holy Spirit.

Jesus' departure made its mark upon the disciples. Many of them testified boldly that Christ had ascended to the Father. As the Jews cast the stones which would take his life, Stephen saw a glorious vision of the Lord in His ascended glory (Acts 7:55-56). Then a short time later, when Saul, the arch-persecutor of the church, made his way to Damascus, he was arrested by the brilliant glory of the same ascended Lord (Acts 9:3-5). So significant was this encounter that Paul twice related the details of his life-changing experience (Acts 22:6-8; 26:13-15). And in an early Christian hymn, Paul unfolds the supreme mystery of the faith, namely that Christ Jesus who "was revealed in the flesh" was at the close of his life "taken up in glory" (1 Tim. 3:16).

Hebrews, more than any other Epistle, underscores the importance of Christ's ascension. The believer's great high priest "has passed through the heavens" into the presence of God (Heb. 4:14). Thinking of the ancient Jewish sanctuary, the writer represents Christ as passing through the veil into the heavenly Holy of Holies (Heb. 6:19) bearing His own blood (Heb. 9:12), that He might "appear in the presence of God for us" (Heb. 9:24).

Critics tend to discredit the Ascension by suggesting that a literal rising involves an antiquated "three-story" view of the universe, with heaven above and hell beneath this earthly plane. They spiritualize the Ascension by suggesting it symbolizes Christ's ascendency over the entire world. We admit that what tonight is over our heads tomorrow will be under our feet. Still, the Ascension did involve a real exit of the God-man from this material world, and a real entrance into God's spiritual world.

Heavenly Session
Following His resurrection from the tomb and ascension to the heavenly realm, Christ took His seat at the Father's right hand. Theologians call this "the session" of Christ. Of course, the biblical phrase, "right hand of God," is a human way of referring to God's universal dominion and power. In Eastern cultures the right hand of the sovereign was a position of honor and authority. So when the Bible says Christ is at God's right hand we know, as Calvin put it, that Christ is "installed in the government of heaven and earth" because the statement, "Christ is seated at God's side" is not suggesting that Jesus is resting from His labor. Rather it points to Christ's reign as King and His exercise of divine power over everyone and everything.

Scripture, however, foretold that Christ would be accorded just such a privilege. The writer of Hebrews applies Psalm 8 specifically to Christ. The words, "Thou hast crowned Him with glory and honor. . . . Thou hast put all things in subjection under His feet"

(Heb. 2:7-8), describes the Saviour's ascension and heavenly session. The same may be said of the Father's command to the Son, "Sit at My right hand, till I make Thine enemies a footstool for Thy feet" (Ps. 110:1).

Toward the end of His earthly life Jesus, knowing this Old Testament background, spoke often of His future exaltation to the throne of heaven. Those who left all and faithfully followed Him, He said, would share in His future reign (Matt. 19:28). In dialogue with the Pharisees shortly before the Cross, Jesus claimed that He was about to ascend to the right hand of the Father (Matt. 22:44). And later before Caiaphas, He spoke boldly of His heavenly reign and glorious return to earth by citing jointly Psalm 110:1 and Daniel 7:13 (Matt. 26:64).

Christ's exalted position at the right hand of God found a central place in the witness of the early church. Peter (Acts 2:33), Stephen (Acts 7:55), and the Apostles generally (Acts 5:31) spoke of Jesus' presence at the Father's side in their evangelistic messages.

In his letters, Paul likewise cited Christ's heavenly session as a sign of God's continual care for His people (Rom. 8:34), as proof of the Son's rule over the universe (Eph. 1:20), and as the source and fount of the church's resurrection life (Col. 3:1).

The Epistle to the Hebrews unfolds Christ's exaltation exclusively in terms of His ascension and heavenly reign. The Lord's resurrection is nowhere in view. The writer's doctrinal interests led him to pass directly from Christ's completed sacrifice on earth to His presence at God's side. So we read in Hebrews 1:3: "When He had made purification of sins, He sat down at the right hand of the Majesty on high" (see also Heb. 12:2).

The letter to the Hebrews also draws an interesting contrast between the ineffectual sacrifices of the traditional Jewish priests who stand while performing their ritual service and the effectual single sacrifice of Christ who is now *seated* at the Father's side (Heb. 10:11-18).

When we come to the Revelation of John we see the Lamb of God in the midst of the throne mediating mercy and grace to the saints (Rev. 7:17). But He is also seen standing by His throne, a posture suited to the execution of judgment upon the earth (Rev. 5:6).

Guarantees of Christ's Ascension and Session

The implications of Christ's elevation to the heavenly throne are far-reaching indeed. What, for example, does it tell us about Christ Himself?

We know that Christ's exaltation to the Father confirms the reality of His divine nature. The Lord spoke of His ascension as a return to a prior dwelling place in heaven (John 6:62; 17:5). Clearly His preexistence with the Father is in view. Paul, too, asserts that at His ascension Christ was proclaimed *Lord,* "to the glory of God the Father" (Phil. 2:11). And we must remember that the title "Lord" here is the New Testament equivalent of the "God" of the Old Testament.

Scripture also regards Christ's ascension and session as the formal inauguration to His high priestly work in heaven. As our Intercessor and Advocate, Christ is the perfect fulfillment of the Aaronic high priest who on the great Day of Atonement, clad in white and bearing the blood, passed within the veil to intercede for the people. During His earthly life Jesus often prayed for others: for small children (Matt. 19:13), for His disciples (Luke 22:31), and even for His enemies (Luke 23:34).

But now the God-man intercedes for His own before the throne of God in heaven (Rom. 8:34). Hebrews teaches that Christ appears before the Father on the believers' behalf (Heb. 9:24), living always "To make intercession for them" (Heb. 7:25). John thinks of Jesus as a lawyer. "If any one does sin, we have an Advocate with the Father, Jesus Christ the righteous" (1 John 2:1). What is an advocate, but one who pleads our case and advances our cause. Billy Graham comments that "Jesus Christ is the Christian's advocate, and He has never lost a case."

Just what does Christ's intercession before the Father's throne accomplish for the believer? All that is necessary for our salvation. In the words of John Owen, the old Puritan divine, Christ's intercession is "His continual appearance for us in the presence of God, representing the efficacy of His oblation, accompanied with tender care and love for the welfare, supply, deliverance, and salvation of the church." Christ died to obtain our salvation; He lives now to maintain us in salvation (Rom. 5:10). There is no truly Christian life without His presence in heaven.

Christ's exaltation to the throne of God is also necessary for the ministry of the Spirit in the church. The Holy Spirit could not be poured out in His fulness until Christ was elevated to glory. In his sermon at Pentecost, Peter explained that the display of the Spirit's power was a direct consequence of Jesus' exaltation to the right hand of God (Acts 2:33-34). When Jesus ascended, His local bodily presence was withdrawn. But when the Holy Spirit descended Christ's spiritual presence was made available to His people anywhere in the world (Matt. 28:20).

This outpouring of the Spirit was important for the church because He bestows grace in the form of spiritual gifts. He gives us to one another so that all believers may attain "the measure of the stature [of the] fulness of Christ" (Eph. 4:13).

Augustine, Bishop of Hippo, once said: "Sons of men, why are you so heavyhearted? Now that Christ the Life has descended to you, why don't you ascend with Him and start living?"

Finally, the ascended Lord is preparing an eternal home for the child of God (John 14:2-3). An ancient legend tells about magic gates that resisted all attempts to force them open. But when one drop of a certain blood fell on them they flung open. So it is that Christ by His own blood has opened for us the gates of heaven. And now He is at work preparing a place for all who love Him.

And the fact that He has entered heaven bodily guarantees that the believer one day shall do the same. Hebrews tells us that Christ has passed through the veil of the heavenly sanctuary as our forerunner (Heb. 6:20). An old Scottish preacher caught the truth when he remarked, "The dust of the earth is on the throne of the majesty on high." Christ has blazed the trail to the heavenly world and the Christian confidently follows in His train.

Christ's Kingly Rule

We saw in Chapter 9 that the kingdom as God's rule or reign arrived in Christ's person and ministry. But our Lord's ascension and authority at the Father's right hand marked a major advance in His kingly rule over the universe. Think of it this way. During the earthly sojourn the King announced His arrival in the palace. But only after His exaltation did He ascend the throne of power and glory. R. L. Dabney notes, "While the Son was permitted to intercede and rule before His incarnation, . . . His kingdom received a still more explicit establishment after His resurrection."

Just before His ascension the One who endured apparent defeat on the cross said to His disciples, "All authority has been given to Me in heaven and on earth" (Matt. 28:18). It was Paul's ministry to unfold this new dimension of Christ's kingly rule. To the Philippians he wrote, "God highly exalted Him, and bestowed on Him the name which is above every name, that at the name of Jesus every knee should bow . . . and that every tongue should confess that Jesus Christ is Lord" (Phil. 2:9-11). The title "Lord" highlights the Sovereign's newly restored authority and dominion.

In a profound sense, then, we may affirm that "Christ is now creation's sceptre-bearer, as He was once creation's burden-bearer" (A. J. Gordon). The Lord rules over a kingdom established not by human blood and steel but by the Spirit of the living God.

The authority of the seated sovereign extends first to all who are of the household of faith. Peter used the analogy of the crown to teach that believers are citizens of Christ's kingdom (2 Peter 1:11). Paul shifted the figure slightly and spoke of Christ as the Head of His body, which is the church (Eph. 1:22; 4:15; Col. 1:18; 2:19). As the head directs the life and activity of the physical body, so Christ sovereignly governs the affairs of His people.

But the ascended and seated Christ also reigns over the world at large. Paul teaches that Christ is "the head over all rule and authority" (Col. 2:10); He is Lord of all because on the cross He disarmed all principalities and powers in anticipation of His final defeat over evil (Col. 2:15). We find the same idea in Peter's letters. As Peter saw it, Christ is Lord of all cosmic agencies. Men, angels, evil powers, even Satan himself are subject to Him (1 Peter 3:22).

Julian the Apostate was a violently anti-Christian Roman emperor who blasphemed the Gospel and persecuted the church. The story is handed down (by Theodoret) that during Julian's campaign against Persia in 363, one of the emperor's soldiers persecuted a Christian in the ranks. The persecutor asked the beleagured man, "Where is your carpenter now?"

The Christian replied, "He is making a coffin for your emperor!"

In a battle a few months' later, Julian received a mortal blow. Rumors circulated in the army that a Christian soldier had inflicted the wound. Realizing that his death was near, Julian dipped his hand in the wound and threw the blood heavenward. As he did he cried out, "O Galilean, Thou hast conquered." The story has a point. Jesus is at the right hand of God creating a coffin for God-rejecting kings and kingdoms of this world. Before long He will destroy them all.

Christ's Second Coming and Eternal Reign

Christ's present reign over the universe is a reality claimed by faith! But the writer to the Hebrews said, "But now we do not yet see all things subjected to Him" (Heb. 2:8). Satan is still loose. He yet roams the earth troubling the saints and opposing the Gospel. The Bible, however, teaches that one day Christ's hidden rule *will* become a visible reality. And that glorious moment will occur at His second coming to earth.

Our Lord promised His followers that He would return. After Jesus spoke of His impending death, He disclosed that He would "come in the glory of His Father with His angels" to visibly establish His kingdom (Matt. 16:27-28). Luke reports that Jesus no sooner ascended into heaven than the promise of His personal return to earth was confirmed by two heavenly messengers (Acts 1:11). Paul (1 Cor. 1:7; 15:23), the writer of Hebrews (9:28), Peter (1 Peter 1:7; 2 Peter 3:3ff.), Jude (v. 14), and John (1 John 2:28; Rev. 1:7) all attest the certainty of Christ's coming again in power.

At an unexpected hour Jesus will return with the suddenness and brilliance of a bolt of lightning flashing across the sky (Matt. 24:29-31). Great cosmic signs will provide the orchestration for the return of the King. Sun and moon will be darkened, heaven and earth will be shaken, and stars will fall from heaven. Christ's second coming opens the door to God's future. Canon Liddon, preaching in London's St. Paul's church, once said, "If Christ is not coming back in glory, then let us turn the key in the west (main) door of this cathedral."

At our Lord's return the dominion inaugurated at His first advent and enlarged at His ascension will become a public reality. "When the Son of Man comes in His glory . . . He will sit on His glorious throne" (Matt. 25:31). The whole world will be summoned before His tribunal. The King will reward believers and punish evildoers (Matt. 25:34, 41). He who crippled Satan at the cross will in that day preside over his final destruction. Death and Hades likewise will be vanquished (Rev. 20:14). At the final victory of the Lamb, the host of heaven will break into a triumphant refrain: "The kingdom of the world has become the kingdom of our Lord, and of His Christ, and He shall reign forever and ever" (Rev. 11:15).

Then the New Jerusalem, the eternal home of the redeemed in Christ, will descend (Rev. 21:2), radiant as a rare jewel. The Holy City will require no temple, "for the Lord God, the Almighty, and the Lamb, are its temple" (Rev. 21:22). Neither will the sun be needed, "for the glory of God has illumined it, and its lamp is the Lamb" (Rev. 21:23). In the new world Christ's servants "shall see His face, and His name shall be on their foreheads" (Rev. 22:4). Then John adds the glorious promise, "and they shall reign forever and ever" (Rev. 22:5).

With the revelation of the new Jerusalem, God's purposes will be complete. Sin and Satan will be destroyed, the saints will enjoy eternal fellowship with God, heaven and earth will be renewed, and the King will exercise absolute sovereignty over a reconciled universe. Light, beauty, holiness, glory, and praise will prevail undisturbed by sin.

Yet the Apocalypse does not close without a final word from the heavenly Lord. "The Spirit and the bride say, 'Come.' And let him who hears say, 'Come.' And let the one who is thirsty come; let the one who wishes take the water of life without cost"

(Rev. 22:17). The promise of a future of eternal glory with Christ includes only one requirement—humble acceptance of His gracious offer of salvation.

> Hark, those bursts of acclamation!
> Hark, those loud triumphant chords!
> Jesus takes the highest station:
> O what joy the sight affords!
> Crown Him! Crown Him!
> King of kings, and Lord of lords!
>
> Thomas Kelly (1769-1854)